the pop classics series

wrapped in plastic.
twin peaks
andy burns

ecwpress

Published by ECW Press
2120 Queen Street East, Suite 200
Toronto, Ontario, Canada M4E 1E2
416-694-3348 / info@ecwpress.com

Editors for the press:
Crissy Calhoun and Jennifer Knoch
Cover and text design: David Gee

Library and Archives Canada
Cataloguing in Publication

Burns, Andy, author
Wrapped in plastic : Twin Peaks /
Andy Burns.

(Pop classics ; 3)
Issued in print and electronic formats.
ISBN 978-1-77041-210-1 (pbk)
Also issued as: 978-1-77090-662-4 (pdf)
978-1-77090-663-1 (ePub)

1. Twin Peaks (Television program). I. Title.

PN1992.77.T88B87 2015   791.45'72
C2014-902539-4   C2014-902540-8

Printing: Webcom   5 4 3 2 1
PRINTED AND BOUND IN CANADA

The publication of *Wrapped in Plastic* has been generously supported by the Canada Council
for the Arts which last year invested $157 million to bring the arts to Canadians throughout
the country, and by the Ontario Arts Council (OAC), an agency of the Government of Ontario,
which last year funded 1,793 individual artists and 1,076 organizations in 232 communities
across Ontario, for a total of $52.1 million. We also acknowledge the financial support of the
Government of Canada through the Canada Book Fund for our publishing activities, and the
contribution of the Government of Ontario through the Ontario Book Publishing Tax Credit and
the Ontario Media Development Corporation.

Ontario
Ontario Media Development
Corporation

ONTARIO ARTS COUNCIL
CONSEIL DES ARTS DE L'ONTARIO
an Ontario government agency
un organisme du gouvernement de l'Ontario

FSC
www.fsc.org

MIX
Paper from
responsible sources
FSC® C004071

Canada Council
for the Arts

Conseil des Arts
du Canada

Canada

To David Lynch and Mark Frost,

for creating the town of Twin Peaks

and

To my mom, for first venturing there

with me all those years ago.

Contents

Introduction

Television in the new millennium can be a glorious place, where boundaries are pushed regularly, often by Hollywood heavyweights. It's where directors such as David Fincher and Martin Scorsese come to experiment with long-form storytelling, and where renowned actors like Kevin Spacey, Jessica Lange, Steve Buscemi, Glenn Close, Kyra Sedgwick, and many others are willing to commit their time and talents. Sometimes there's the allure of a great story that can be told in one season (an enticement that drew bona fide movie stars Woody Harrelson and Matthew McConaughey to HBO's *True Detective*). Other times, there's the appeal of both creativity and freedom (Kevin Bacon only has to shoot 15 episodes a season of Fox's *The Following*, allowing him to pursue big screen roles while also enjoying a steady paycheck). With the advent of edgy original programming across networks like AMC, Showtime, FX, Netflix, and HBO, the appeal of working in television has never been higher.

It wasn't always like this, though. For decades, television

was a training ground for new faces rather than a destination for proven talent. In the 1980s, cable networks had yet to establish themselves as centers of creative activity, and instead mainly filled their airwaves with movies and syndicated reruns. Occasionally you'd see a big name attach themselves to a network show (Steven Spielberg worked with NBC on the anthology series *Amazing Stories*, which ran for two interesting yet largely ignored seasons between 1985 and 1987), but for the most part, television was home to standard-fare sitcoms, dramas, and nighttime soap operas of varied quality, driven by TV veterans rather than cinematic auteurs.

Then David Lynch showed up.

Collaborating with Mark Frost, a well-regarded writer who'd worked on the critically and commercially successful television series *Hill Street Blues*, Lynch hit upon a concept that could actually work in a serialized, episodic format. It would be a murder mystery: the tale of Laura Palmer (Sheryl Lee), a popular high school girl found murdered, her body washed up on the beach. Wrapped in plastic.

Enter earnest FBI Special Agent Dale Cooper (Kyle MacLachlan), sent to investigate Laura's death and unravel an increasingly complex and bizarre case.

The basic story was far from original. But in the hands of two visionary creators like David Lynch and Mark Frost, *Twin Peaks* took the familiar and transformed it into a series no one could have anticipated.

Amid a network schedule that included shows such as *Roseanne*, *Who's the Boss?*, and *thirtysomething*, *Twin Peaks* debuted on ABC on Sunday, April 8, 1990, in a two-hour movie-length episode written by Lynch and Frost, and directed by Lynch himself. Nearly 35 million people viewed the premiere, no doubt the biggest audience the notoriously avant-garde David Lynch had ever had for any of his work. Critics were immediately enthusiastic: *Entertainment Weekly*'s Ken Tucker gave the premiere an A+, while the *Washington Post*'s Jen Chaney called it "one of the most finely crafted series kick-offs in broadcast history."

When it moved into its Thursdays at 9 p.m. timeslot, *Twin Peaks* did lose some viewers — not unexpectedly, as it was up against the NBC comedy juggernaut *Cheers*. However, it still maintained a large audience that was enthralled with the quirky inhabitants of this small Northwest American town, even as the weird touches that were hallmarks of David Lynch's style increased in frequency. After a short run of eight episodes, the first season of *Twin Peaks* concluded with a Mark Frost–directed episode full of cliffhangers that left audiences debating not only "Who killed Laura Palmer?" but "Who shot Agent Cooper?" — both slogans that made it onto the requisite t-shirts. I still have mine in a box someplace.

I was 13 years old that summer and, sitting alongside my mother, I voraciously consumed every episode of *Twin Peaks*. ("You were way too young to be watching that show, my dear," Sheryl Lee told me with a laugh some 24 years later.) Since I was already a fan of supernatural stories in film and literature, the strangeness that permeated the show captured my imagination. During the wait for the second season, I debated the ins and outs of the series with Mom and a few friends, trying to unravel the multiple mysteries we'd been left to ponder.

As summer 1990 turned to fall, *Twin Peaks* mania showed no signs of letting up. Series star Kyle MacLachlan hosted the season premiere of *Saturday Night Live*, while starlets Mädchen Amick, Sherilyn Fenn, and Lara Flynn Boyle graced the cover of *Rolling Stone*. *The Secret Diary of Laura Palmer*, penned by Lynch's daughter Jennifer at age 22, was a *New York Times* bestseller, and the show's soundtrack, by composer Angelo Badalamenti, made the Billboard charts and went on to win a Grammy. Damn good coffee and cherry pie were all the rage and, for a brief moment in time, David Lynch was the unexpected face of network television.

It couldn't last. And it didn't. Almost as quickly as it had risen to the top of the Nielsen ratings, *Twin Peaks* managed to lose the bulk of its audience. The first signs of trouble came with its second-season premiere, which aired on Sunday, September 30, 1990, against a Perry Mason movie-of-the-week on NBC. Though "May the Giant Be With You" (2.01) still garnered nearly 20 million viewers, it came in second to Raymond Burr's venerable and much older-skewing lawyer. Not a good sign.

From there, *Twin Peaks* settled uncomfortably into another new timeslot — 10 p.m. on Saturday nights, a dreaded wasteland for episodic television. ABC had hoped that the hype around the show's must-see first season would translate to viewers on a night that rarely had any, but it didn't. The audience that originally embraced *Twin Peaks* actually went out on Saturday nights, and in an era before DVRs, the ratings dropped alarmingly week to week. Meanwhile, those who did tune in regularly were anxious for Laura Palmer's killer to be revealed, something David Lynch and Mark Frost hadn't planned on doing — at least, not so soon. However, bowing to network pressure and diminishing returns, the duo bit the bullet, baby. On Saturday, November 10, 1990, 17 million people watched one of the most horrific revelations in television history: Laura Palmer's anguished father, Leland (Ray Wise), possessed by the evil spirit BOB, had killed her. It was shocking. It was upsetting. It was pure David Lynch.

It was too late.

With the mystery finally solved in a manner few could have anticipated, and without an ongoing storyline to captivate audiences, the show that had been lauded for its innovative storytelling and style plunged even further in the ratings. (Frequent preemptions because of the Gulf War didn't help matters either.) By the time *Twin Peaks* was canceled toward the end of its second season, barely nine million people were watching. Those of us who stuck around to the last episode were taunted with a cliffhanger that was never resolved.

Countless other short-lived series have floated off into the ether of network television history. But like the best art, not only has *Twin Peaks* never really gone away, it continues to find a new audience. Fans gather annually, websites are devoted to its characters and settings, video games have been inspired by it. There was even a long-running fanzine that meticulously delved into all sorts of *Twin Peaks* and Lynch ephemera, with which this book proudly shares a title. And then, in October

2014, after years of denials Lynch and Frost revealed that they were returning to Twin Peaks with a nine-episode series to run on Showtime.

Twin Peaks has been resurrected but the art of television itself had already been irrevocably changed by the show. A program that many perceived as too weird and as a commercial failure became one of the most influential television series of the past 25 years with just 30 episodes. Nothing is ever as it seems on *Twin Peaks*, and audiences continue to respond to that feeling of disorientation amidst the familiar. The show's storytelling sensibility, visual language, and quirky tone were once foreign to network television; its most impressive trick was to ensnare audiences with the familiar — namely, nighttime soap opera tropes — before venturing off into the uncharted: taboo subject matter, supernatural dream worlds both hypnotic and horrifying, secrets and double identities. A fish in the percolator.

By wrapping their work in the plastic of conventional television storytelling, and then reimagining what the medium could deliver, David Lynch and Mark Frost redefined the boundaries of network TV, creating one of the most influential series in the history of the medium; one that, for a brief moment in time, enthralled an audience that hadn't known they were hungry for something new until they finally got a taste.

Welcome to Twin Peaks.

1

"What is it you do, exactly?"

At the dawn of the 1990s, I was a 13-year-old kid growing up in suburban Toronto, obsessed with the music of the 1960s and 1970s — the Rolling Stones, the Doors, and Pink Floyd. Elvis Presley and the Everly Brothers were ancient artifacts of a forgotten time. The 1950s seemed like another world entirely, a fantasy place I recognized only thanks to the occasional *Happy Days* rerun and an enduring love of *Back to the Future*. Though I was an avid *Twin Peaks* fan, I didn't realize then that the Double R Diner was a throwback to the malt shops of the past. I didn't view Special Agent Dale Cooper as a modern day G-man, nor did I recognize brooding and pouting biker James Hurley as an embodiment of the iconic greaser of the '50s. As James Marshall, who portrayed the character, told me in 2014, at the time of casting "[Lynch] was looking for what they called the 'James Dean type' . . . the gentleman who was representing me back then, funny enough, was the guy who discovered James Dean." The other teens in *Twin Peaks*, the Audrey Hornes and Donna Haywards, dressed like they'd just walked off *American Bandstand*, as though the past 40 years hadn't occurred. On *Twin Peaks*, time often appears to have stood still. While the teen me might have missed it, the 34 million viewers of the show's pilot likely didn't.

The 1950s had been a pivotal point for American pop culture. World War II was over and the Cold War had yet to instill fear in the nation. While the early part of the decade found the crooners of the '40s still thriving with adult listeners, the mid-1950s saw the advent of rock and roll — Elvis, Buddy Holly, Bill Haley and his Comets, to name but a few. Parents recoiled while their children embraced the rhythmic sounds of distorted guitar, bass, and drums (music occasionally used as part of the *Twin Peaks* soundtrack alongside composer Angelo Badalamenti's moody score). Then there was the medium of television itself, which had entered the homes of millions of Americans. In 1948, only 350,000 homes in the U.S. were fitted with TVs. Five years later, that number had leaped to 25,000,000 — nearly 50% of all homes in the country.[1] *The Honeymooners, I Love Lucy, Leave It to Beaver, The Adventures of Ozzie and Harriet*: all became part of the culture zeitgeist. These were the shows Americans gathered in front of their televisions to watch, welcoming idyllic family values into their homes every night. Canadian sociologist and futurist Marshall McLuhan once said, "All media exist to invest our lives with artificial perceptions and arbitrary values." In the 1950s, television became a common bond for people, breaking into the cultural consciousness by giving audiences an ideal to strive for.

David Keith Lynch was born in Missoula, Montana, in 1946, but moved around the United States thanks to his father's job for the Department of Agriculture. Unsurprisingly, his father's occupation helped give Lynch his ongoing love of the outdoors, which manifests itself in Lynch's surrogate on *Twin Peaks*, Special Agent Dale Cooper. ("Got to find out what kind of trees these are; they're really something," dictates Cooper on his first drive into town.) While the constant movement and upheaval in Lynch's life could have been cause for grief or discontent, the truth was, unlike many of the characters in his art, David Lynch was raised in a loving and supportive environment. In his own words, the 1950s world he grew up in seemed perfect; it was what lay underneath that perfection where he would ultimately find his inspiration.

"My childhood was elegant homes, tree-lined streets, the milkman, building backyard forts, droning airplanes, blue skies, picket fences, green grass, cherry trees," Lynch told Chris Rodley for his book *Lynch on Lynch*. "Middle America as it's supposed to be. But on the cherry tree there's this pitch oozing out — some black, some yellow, and millions of red ants crawling all over it. I discovered that if one looks a little closer at this beautiful world, there are always red ants underneath. Because I grew up in a perfect world, other things were a contrast."[2]

In its exploration of the darkness under the light of

day-to-day living, Lynch's 1986 film *Blue Velvet* serves as a spiritual prequel to *Twin Peaks*. *Blue Velvet* is the story of Jeffrey Beaumont (Kyle MacLachlan), who discovers a severed human ear while walking through a field in his hometown. Jeffrey is swept into the world lurking underneath his neighborhood's harmless exterior, one full of psychotic criminals and violent sex — topics the director continued to explore with *Twin Peaks*. Dark and disturbing, with moments of uncomfortable humor that sneak up on the viewer, the film also manages to celebrate the '50s iconography that David Lynch so loves — Laura Dern's retro skirt–wearing teen queen, Sandy Williams, could have easily fit in at Twin Peaks High School, while the film's soundtrack makes outstanding use of two '50s standards, Roy Orbison's "In Dreams" and the film's title song, seductively crooned by Lynch's then-paramour and the movie's femme fatale (another hallmark of film and literature of the era), Isabella Rossellini. Leading into the creation of *Twin Peaks*, the decade of Lynch's youth clearly had a hold on his imagination.

A few years younger than Lynch, Mark Frost, born in 1953 in Brooklyn and raised in Los Angeles, California, found his inspiration from more conventional fare. "I was initially swept away by classic adventure authors like James Fenimore Cooper, H.G. Wells, Jules Verne, H. Rider Haggard," he recalled in 2012. "As I got older, I got a little more populist in my tastes and embraced pulp fiction like Doc Savage and Tarzan. I also became a comic book collector in my early teenage years, particularly the Silver Age of the Marvel Universe and that led me into Tolkien and fantasy and sci-fi like Heinlein, Le Guin, and Bradbury."[3] Frost's love of sci-fi continued with his discovery of *The Prisoner*, the late 1960s British television show about a secret agent held in a seemingly idyllic seaside village alongside others whose names, like the agent's, have been replaced with numbers. According to Frost, the psychedelic, spooky, and oftentimes just plain weird show "was very formative for me as a kid; it gave me the courage to go in different directions from a narrative standpoint."[4]

The young Frost also developed a taste for 1940s and '50s film noir, which came in handy during the three years he spent as a writer on the critically acclaimed and commercially successful NBC crime drama *Hill Street Blues* (1981–1987), itself inspired by the police procedural novels that first gained popularity in the 1950s. Frost made his bones working alongside brilliant writers like show creator Stephen Bochco and future TV series creators Anthony Yerkovich (*Miami Vice*) and David Milch (*NYPD Blue*, *Deadwood*). During *Hill Street Blues*'s seven-season run, the writers broke ground by using slang and common language to lend the series a more authentic feel. It was also one of the first nighttime network shows that was narratively complex — storylines intertwined and could last the length of a season, instead of only an episode. As Frost later recalled to Sean Morrow, "The experience on *Hill Street Blues* taught me about multiple story arcs on a broad network scale."

According to a story Mark Frost told in 2013 to a crowd gathered at the University of Southern California for a *Twin Peaks* retrospective, when he and Lynch first met, they immediately connected and began exploring ideas, none of them taking off. "And then [CAA agent and future *Mulholland Drive* producer] Tony [Krantz] called us up one day and asked us if we wanted to do a TV show," recalled Frost. "And we said heck no!"

Neither Lynch nor Frost had any interest in collaborating on a television series. While Frost may have thrived writing *Hill Street Blues*, the ideas he and Lynch had been crafting were designed for the silver screen. They shared a rebellious mentality seemingly unsuited to the confines of network television. As Frost recalled, "David and I always had this feeling of ourselves as outsiders. Even though I'd done three years on *Hill Street Blues* and had worked in kind of mainstream television during that period, I never felt like I had ever been embraced by the mainstream. I wasn't too interested in that."[5]

Lynch's work had been based in the limitless potential of film — not to mention everything an R rating would allow. His first film, 1977's *Eraserhead*, was a nightmarish, surreal head trip about a man caring for his deformed child. No studio would touch the film, which found its fame on the midnight movie circuit, where it became a cult favorite. His second, 1980's *The Elephant Man*, told the true tale of the deformed 19th-century Englishman Joseph Merrick. The film was nominated for eight Academy Awards, including one for Best Director, though it won none. With the exception of his third film, 1984's sci-fi would-be epic *Dune*, which had courted and failed to find a mainstream audience, Lynch's movies had been dark, art-house projects. At the end of the '80s, television was seen as a stepping-stone to the more artistic and lucrative world of moviemaking; why would David Lynch want to work in a limiting medium?

However, Tony Krantz kept encouraging Frost and Lynch to consider the possibility. At a Los Angeles restaurant called Nibblers, Krantz suggested Lynch "do a show about real life in America, [Lynch's] vision of America the same way [he] demonstrated in *Blue Velvet*."[6] A small town setting struck a nerve, and Lynch and Frost began to see its potential. The duo started throwing around a few ideas. Recalling the 1957 film *Peyton Place*, about a New England town rife with sex, murder, and moral ambiguity, Frost liked the idea of focusing on multiple lives in a small community where outside appearances mask something darker, revealed only behind closed doors. Lynch became interested in the storytelling possibilities television could offer. "A continuing story is a beautiful thing to me," Lynch told *Entertainment Weekly* in 2000. "And a mystery is a beautiful thing to me, so if you have a continuing mystery, it's so beautiful. And you can go deeper into a story and discover so many things."[7]

David Lynch and Mark Frost soon hit upon the simple image they would pitch to Chad Hoffman, ABC's vice president for dramatic series, in a 10-minute meeting: a woman's corpse wrapped in plastic washed ashore in a small town — the homecoming queen murdered. While the murder, and the character's dark secret life, would be the catalyst for the series, the plan was for that story to move into the background as the audience got to know the eclectic citizens of the town.

When Lynch and Frost eventually handed in the finished pilot to ABC, its head honcho, Robert Iger, ordered an additional seven episodes. But most of the studio executives weren't sure what to make of *Twin Peaks*. As one unnamed executive prophetically said at the time, "Most people here do not expect that *Twin Peaks* will work. The critics and audiences give us signals like 'We're tired of what we've seen before; don't give us more of the same.' But when you venture out there, there are not a lot of indications that they're embracing what's different. It's like a wife-mistress thing. 'Yeah, we wanna get it down and dirty, I want that choice in my life, but I wanna come home to a good mother.' In some ways, maybe what David will be is the martyr who will push the boundaries — expand what TV can do and should do — without being wholly successful."[8] Lynch and Frost did indeed push the boundaries of television, finding a new audience, while also appealing to the one already familiar with Lynch's work in cinema. "When [David Lynch] came to television, there was no way I wasn't going to watch," said actor James Roday, who at 14 years old in 1990 was already a Lynch fan and would, more than 20 years later, spearhead a tribute episode to *Twin Peaks* on his own series, *Psych*. "Of course, he delivered everything that you would expect David Lynch to deliver, and more, and he was doing it in primetime network television."[9]

2

"A place both wonderful and strange"

Our first taste of *Twin Peaks* comes in its alluring opening credits. Unlike shows like *Dallas* or *Beverly Hills, 90210*, where actors' images and clips from episodes are given the most screen time, the opening credits to *Twin Peaks* set the mood by showing us the town — the sawmill, smoke emanating from its stacks; a Welcome to Twin Peaks sign; a river tinged with dark water calmly running. The credits take their time, a minute and a half, to transport viewers into the strange town in a visually memorable calling card, a gateway into the world that David Lynch and Mark Frost have created. The visual is complemented by the gorgeous series theme, written by Angelo Badalamenti. There are no clever lyrics (though singer Julee Cruise later recorded a version with words penned by David Lynch), no trumpets blaring or rock and roll guitar riffs. Only a slow moving instrumental that swells just as the show's title appears onscreen. Though there's nothing flashy or sexy about the series opening, it's haunting in its focus. The Great Northern Hotel, the Packard Sawmill, the forest and sprawling trees that first capture the interest of Agent Cooper — they're all here in these opening moments, conveyed in a serene yet foreboding manner. This combination of images and music is much closer to an opening sequence of a film than the typical television show. As audiences would soon find out, *Twin Peaks* was anything but typical.

Before crafting any of the characters who would inhabit *Twin Peaks*, David Lynch and Mark Frost first nailed down the small-town setting. They drew a map and established town landmarks, such as the omnipresent mill seen during the show's opening credits. Creating a believable location outside the sprawl of Hollywood wasn't difficult for either man, since both had grown up away from urban environments — Frost spending his formative years in Minnesota, while Lynch traveled with his family throughout the Northwest and lived in towns like Spokane, Washington, and Boise, Idaho, during his boyhood. When shooting began on the *Twin Peaks* pilot, it took place throughout Washington State, where the lush green forests, cascading waterfalls, and small towns seemed transported directly out of Lynch's childhood memories.

In a bit of cosmic good fortune, while Lynch and Frost were scouting locations, a friend's recommendation led them to Snoqualmie Falls, Washington, which, to their amazement, was the spitting image of what they had written in their pilot. "There was a little diner across from the railroad station," Frost recalled in 2000. "There was the sawmill right in town. There was what looked like, in our minds, the Great Northern Hotel on the hill overlooking the town perched next to a waterfall. It was a really weird moment of synchronicity."[10] This manifestation of what Lynch and Frost had come up with on paper would be the first of many surprises that the series embraced in its two-season run.

As a filmmaker, David Lynch is always open to inspiration and improvisation, a sensibility uncommon on a network dramatic series, but one that allowed for moments of inspired madness in *Twin Peaks*. As part of the deal struck with ABC, David Lynch shot a closed ending to the pilot of *Twin Peaks* for the European market so that if the network chose not to pick up the show, they would at least be able to release it as a proper film with an actual ending. It was in preparing this sequence (in which Laura's killer is a drifter) that Lynch dreamt up the Red Room. As the director explained in *Lynch on Lynch*, "I was leaning against a car — the front of me was leaning against this very warm car. My hands were on the roof and the metal was very hot. The Red Room scene leapt into my mind. 'Little Mike' was there, and he was speaking backwards . . . For the rest of the night I thought only about the Red Room."[11]

The Red Room, first shown in "Zen, or the Skill to Catch a Killer" (1.03), initially seemed to serve no distinct purpose — was it art for art's sake? As Michael J. Anderson, who portrayed the Man from Another Place, explains, "There was *no* explanation of the scene, whatsoever. I presented [Lynch] with an interpretation of the scene to which he got a sour look and said, 'No, no that's not it at all. Do you still think that?' 'I guess not.' 'Okay then, we're ready to shoot.' He would just wipe away any concept I had and then replace it with nothing. One time I asked, 'David, what is the context of this scene? What happens before or after this?' 'Well, Mike, this scene doesn't have any context. There is no before or after this scene.' At the time, it made me angry because how can there be a scene without context? But when I saw the finished product, he was right. The scene floated in mid-air, with no linear context. He was telling the truth, I just couldn't grasp it."[12]

Like Anderson, when audiences first entered the Red Room, they had no context for what they were experiencing — an art house moment had busted into the living rooms of America. It was weird and surreal and jarring and unexplainable; *Twin Peaks* was definitely more than just a murder mystery thanks to its alluring visuals, amusing quirks, and hint of the supernatural. With this dream sequence alone, *Twin Peaks* cemented itself as unlike anything ever before seen in popular media. Reviews since have referred to the scene as "some of the most disquieting filmmaking Lynch has ever done,"[13] while also labeling the episode as a whole "the best in the series, the one that turned *Twin Peaks* into a water-cooler phenomenon."[14] The Red Room became, and 25 years later remains, *Twin Peaks'* pop-culture calling card.

The figure of BOB came to *Twin Peaks* in a serendipitous moment that another director may have simply disregarded as a mistake. Prepping for a scene in Laura's bedroom, a set dresser named Frank Silva was moving furniture around and was warned by a colleague not to trap himself in the room. "I wasn't even looking in [his] direction," said Lynch. "But the image of Frank locked in that room popped into my head, and I rushed to Frank and I said, 'Frank, are you an actor?' And he said, 'Why yes, I happen to be.' And I said, 'You're going to be in this movie.'"[15] Without having a particular use in mind for the shot, but willing to simply embrace its *potential* (a virtue also possessed by Agent Cooper), Lynch then filmed the longhaired, denim-clad Silva crouched down at the foot of Laura's bed, staring through the bedframe directly at the camera. Hours later, Lynch was filming another scene in the Palmer house: a bereaved Sarah Palmer (Grace Zabriskie) is lying on her couch, smoking a cigarette, when she is terrified by a ghastly vision. Lynch was satisfied with the take; however, a mirror had accidentally caught the reflection of one of the set crew, and Lynch was informed they'd have to do it again. When the director asked who was in the shot, it turned out to be none other than Frank Silva. This would be one of those fortuitous, happy accidents that David Lynch often embraces; not only did Silva's reflection stay in the scene, he became BOB, a drifter in the European version and, in the series, the supernatural embodiment of the evil that surrounds the town of Twin Peaks.

Working in television didn't stop David Lynch from using techniques usually reserved for the big screen. In typical TV visual language, long or wide shots were used primarily to establish a setting: a scene opens with a shot of a location from a considerable distance, then cuts into closer framing, so the actors fill up the screen. Lynch, however, chose a different approach during one of the pilot's most significant moments — the first meeting between Agent Cooper and Sheriff Truman (Michael Ontkean). We're looking down to the end of a long hallway. Cooper enters the scene from the left, Truman from the right, and they meet in the middle. We watch from a distance as they shake hands, but because they're far away, we can't make out their faces. The camera is still as the two turn and begin to walk toward us, but as they get closer it tracks along with Cooper and Truman until they stop and converse again, as Cooper explains that the FBI will be in charge of the murder investigation, not the Twin Peaks Sheriff's Department. In this instance, the audience is virtually eavesdropping on their conversation. We're placed at a distance, analogous to Cooper's anticipated relationship with local law enforcement. As we get closer, so do the men, foreshadowing the bond they'll eventually share. This FBI-versus–local PD dynamic is already off-kilter, the familiar presented through a different lens.

Along with long shots, unusual close-ups abound throughout the series. We first experience them in the pilot, when we're privy to a prime moment of Lynchian discomfort, a hallmark of the director's work. For instance, in *Blue Velvet*, when Kyle MacLachlan's character discovers a severed ear lying in a field, the audience is treated to a close-up shot of the appendage, bruised and covered by crawling ants. Instead of being a gross-out moment, it's essential to the story and beautifully composed. In *Twin Peaks*, it's once again MacLachlan's job to guide the viewer through disturbing imagery. At the Twin Peaks morgue, Cooper discovers something underneath one of Laura Palmer's fingernails. The camera closes in on two hands — Cooper's and Laura's. With a pair of tweezers, Cooper probes and digs deep beneath the nail of Laura's corpse-blue ring finger. While not a violent image, it's uncomfortable and disconcerting for the viewer, the character and the camera both venturing into morbid territory. Though there are two brief cutaways (one to Truman's puzzled face, the other to Cooper's determined look), the moment lasts more than ten seconds. From underneath the nail, Cooper retrieves a minuscule piece of paper marked with the letter R. This was the one scene in the pilot that the network had issues with, requesting it be edited, but Frost and Lynch didn't capitulate. The scene went to air as its creators wished, an uncompromised moment in an uncompromising television series.

One of *Twin Peaks'* more remarkable achievements was how it managed to make seemingly harmless and mundane inanimate objects frightening, and not just via extreme or jarring close-ups. Take the traffic light swinging in the wind, used frequently throughout the series as an insert shot transitioning between scenes. David Lynch explained that particular recurring motif, which first appears in the pilot episode: "Well, the intersection of Sparkwood and 21 was where Laura last saw James — or James last saw Laura. And these traffic lights are there. Snow and different temperatures mean that they have to be fluid. So they blow in the wind. And those traffic lights become kind of important. They were used again where Cooper says [in the pilot], 'All those murders took place at night.' So when you see this red light, or a light turning to red, and it's moving, it gives you a feeling. And then it becomes like the fan in the hall outside Laura's room. It makes you wonder. And it gives you the willies!"[16] The ceiling fan Lynch is referring to appears in the pilot and again in *Twin Peaks: Fire Walk with Me*, shot on an upward angle to imbue the object with a feeling of power and importance. Add in the sound of the fan spinning, and it becomes a symbol of dread. It's clear from the pilot that something horrible is associated with the spinning fan, a point proven when it is revealed that Leland/BOB would turn on the fan prior to raping Laura in her bedroom. In "Lonely Souls" (2.07), the fan runs as Leland/BOB drugs his wife and murders his niece (and to make the scene even more circular, a record player continuously spins, though no music emanates from it). In the prequel film, Leland/BOB turns on the fan prior to his final rape of his daughter, who looks up when she hears it begin spinning. Laura knows something horrible is coming. The cycle of violence continues. This has happened before. It is happening again.

Even dresser drawers take on a sinister aspect. In one of the series' more cryptic moments, Josie Packard (Joan Chen) dies in the final scene of "The Condemned Woman" (2.16), of apparent heart failure in a room at the Great Northern Hotel, after shooting her longtime associate Thomas Eckhardt (David Warner). The episode ends with an image of Josie's face confined within a dresser drawer knob; what could be interpreted as her soul is trapped within it, writhing to get free. In the hands of Lynch and company, these objects evoke an emotional response in the viewer, the everyday and inanimate becoming associated with the horrific.

Along with his unique visual sensibility, David Lynch is also in command of a manner with talent — from the audition room through to his interactions on set — that transcends the usual actor/director relationship. In all of the episodes of *Twin Peaks* that he directed — "Pilot" (1.01), "Zen, or the Skill to Catch a Killer" (1.03), "May the Giant Be with You" (2.01), "Coma" (2.02), "Lonely Souls" (2.07), and "Beyond Life and Death" (2.22) — his approach was primarily about connection, a mentality that his actors found refreshing.

Kimmy Robertson, who played Lucy Moran, recalls, "The way David Lynch worked with me was he would get everyone to sit down somewhere quiet and then say, 'Alright, so, Lucy, now, the phone's going to ring in the scene and the Sheriff's going to be nearby. Now, you are the center of the centrifuge of Twin Peaks. You know everything that's going on. Your nose is into everything but only because you want to help the Sheriff and make sure that everybody's safe. You don't just use one carbon paper, you use two and three — triplicate so you've got plenty of backup.' He went on like that for a little while and I'm sitting there and he's sitting next to me with his hand on my knee or on my shoulder sometimes. I know that he had to touch me so that he could get this magic message into the cellular structure of my body. He absolutely knew what he was

23

doing. And his daughter does the exact same thing. I've never worked with anybody else who does it quite like them. He magnetizes everybody to be on the same page."[17]

Robertson's co-star Dana Ashbrook, who played Bobby Briggs, concurs: "He's completely different in the way he would approach direction. He'll tell you a dream he had or a feeling or [about] a music piece, and give you the vibe that way. He's more apt to be ethereal in his direction, which makes it so fun and beautiful — a fun place to hang out. He was the kind of guy that would do anything for you. He'd tell you to do any sort of thing and you'd do it, trusting that it would come out funny or cool or interesting. You go with that sort of trust, because he was such a kind and affable guy, eccentric and interesting and fascinating."[18] One emotional moment between Ashbrook's Bobby and the character's father, Major Briggs (Don Davis), during "May the Giant Be with You" (2.01), is a prime example of Lynch's style of directing. According to Ashbrook, "That [scene] was actually written with Bobby not going either way emotionally. I went to Mark Frost and he said, 'No, Bobby is not into it and he's just irritated by his dad.' And I was like, 'Oh okay, I get it.' And then when we got on the set, David was like, 'No, no, no! It's completely the opposite.' [laughs] We did Don's lines first. I was just listening to the story that he was doing and he was so good. And then they turned around on me, and David wanted me to cry but it wasn't really working. And instead of talking to me, David took Don aside and he talked to *him*. Don came back and while we did the scene, Don started crying off-camera. When he started crying, *I* started crying."

Twin Peaks' infamous leading corpse, Sheryl Lee, remembers Lynch's style of directing fondly. "There was a scene on the TV series where I was playing Maddy, and I was sitting in the diner with Lara [Flynn Boyle]," says Lee. "And it was cold and rainy and we were drinking coffee. And David's direction was along the lines of 'Okay, it's 1950 and it's summer and you're drinking milkshakes.' Well, it wasn't 1950, it wasn't summer, and we *weren't* drinking milkshakes. But he goes and tells this whole thing and then says, 'Action!' Now, if you're going to try and make sense of that with your logical mind, you're not going to be present in the moment. But if you surrender to wherever it is he's taking you, then by the time he says action, you realize that he has taken you somewhere. He's taken you exactly where he wants to take you, and he starts the scene from that place. It's like a brushstroke that he's just painted across you. And then, when you're in the world with him for a while, you get that this man really is brilliant.

"He creates an environment that is so safe, and you know that you can jump off that cliff because there are calm, still waters at the bottom. He's very supportive, and you want to do your best for him. You want to give him everything you have creatively because he is so brilliant. I trust his vision."[19]

In an interview with Brad Dukes for the Twin Peaks Archive website, Lee also recalled just how meticulous David Lynch was as a director. "David is such an artist," she said. "You know when you see that picture of me with plastic wrapped around my face and the sand particles? David placed those sand particles. David placed the plastic. David knew exactly what color my skin had to be and worked with the make-up artists. He is a true visual artist in that sense, as well as being a director. He knew what image he wanted to portray, down to the folds of the plastic. So, I really felt a lot like his canvas in that sense for all the dead scenes."[20]

It's worth noting here that while David Lynch's style is inimitable, none of the other directors who worked on *Twin Peaks* were forced or encouraged to try to ape the man. "They have a script and they chat with one or both of us and away they go," recalled David Lynch. "And then I'd see their shows at the sound mix. If something was completely wrong, there would be time to fix it. But I can't say that ever happened."[21] According to Mark Frost, "I said to everyone who came in, 'Please don't feel obligated to imitate a house style. There are parameters to work with and a vocabulary we'd like to use, but we want you to feel like you have the freedom to shoot the episode the way you want to shoot it.'"[22] In another interview, Frost further discussed their parameters. "What I would tell directors coming in was to study the pilot, look at the story-telling style we've evolved here, and figure out what you can bring to it," he recalled. "We were hiring really talented and interesting people and I didn't want them to just come in and feel like they're stamping out engine parts at a Chrysler plant. I think everyone understood that was the assignment: work with the house style and the mood that David had so brilliantly created and then bring whatever you can of yourself to add to that; and I would say nine times out of ten that worked out really well."[23] The one out of ten led to humorous stories, such as when German filmmaker Uli Edel was asked to direct "Double Play" (2.14). Edel had impressed North American critics with his 1989 adaptation of the classic Hubert Selby Jr. novel *Last Exit to Brooklyn*. Unfortunately, for some *Twin Peaks* actors, Edel's style missed the mark.

"[There was a scene where] Robyn Lively [who played Southern belle Lana Budding Milford] had all the men in the office at the Sheriff's station," recalled Kimmy Robertson. "And Uli had the camera turning sideways. First he has a fisheye lens on, and then he has it turned sideways. He has the handheld camera guy turning sideways and then coming back up and then turning sideways the other way. Michael Ontkean says, 'Uli, why?' and he says, 'Because it's *Twin Peaks*! It's weird! Everything here is weird! I'm going to make it weirder!' And it's, like, that doesn't make any sense. It's not weird for weird's sake."[24]

For its actors and its creators, *Twin Peaks* was about allowing for inspiration and intuition to move in any variety of creative directions. Not to force silliness or weirdness, but to be open to whatever spirit moved the artist. The various directors who made their way through *Twin Peaks* were not only allowed to use their own visual approaches, they were also more than happy to learn a few lessons from David Lynch himself. In a 2013 interview, Lesli Linka Glatter, who directed four episodes of the series — "Cooper's Dreams" (1.06), "The Man Behind Glass" (2.03), "Demons" (2.06), and "The Condemned Woman" (2.16) — recalled talking to David Lynch about the hilarious moment in the pilot episode when, at the Twin Peaks

Bank, a moose head is on a conference room table that Cooper and Sheriff Truman need to use. Nobody says a word about what's in front of their faces; they simply go about their business as if there was nothing out of the ordinary.

"So, when I got to know David," recalled Glatter, "I went up to him and said, 'How did you ever get the idea to put the moose head on the table?' He looked at me like I was kind of crazy, and he said, 'It was there.' And I said, 'What do you mean it was there?' He said, 'The set decorator was going to hang it on the wall,' and David said to the decorator, 'Leave the moose head.' Something just cracked open in my brain: be sure you're open to the moment. Be sure you see the moose head on the table. Don't try to control things so much that you're not open to what's happening in the moment. That was a great lesson and a huge turning point for me."[25]

Many of the directors who passed through *Twin Peaks* managed to create some gorgeous art of their own while working on Lynch and Frost's turf. Noted cinematographer Caleb Deschanel — who had previously been nominated for Academy Awards for *The Right Stuff* (1983) and *The Natural* (1984) and whose wife, Mary Jo, was cast as Donna Hayward's mother, Eileen — directed three episodes of the series: "Realization Time" (1.07), "The Black Widow" (2.12), and "Drive with a Dead Girl" (2.08), where he was given the unenviable task of following "Lonely Souls" (2.07), the Lynch-directed episode that revealed Laura's killer. At the USC *Twin Peaks* Retrospective in March 2013, Deschanel recalled suggesting to Lynch that, during a scene where an imprisoned Benjamin Horne (Richard Beymer) and his lawyer brother Jerry (David Patrick Kelly) recall a dance their baby-sitter Louise Dombrowski (Emily Fincher) once performed for them, we actually flash back to the moment, with a young Ben and Jerry gleefully smiling as Louise, her face hidden in the shadows, alluringly dances. Deschanel's suggestion made the finished episode, a gorgeously filmed memory offering up a brief respite for the jailed Ben Horne, a scene that feels distinctly *Twin Peaks*.

Annie Hall herself, Diane Keaton, was behind the lens for "Slaves and Masters" (2.15), an episode many fans consider the nadir of the entire series; mind you, this was more because of the ongoing season two scripting issues than Keaton's directorial abilities. The episode itself makes use of the required windswept tree inserts, while also utilizing some not-so-subtle slow-motion techniques that fit right into the language of the series. Keaton even managed to demonstrate a somewhat Lynchian willingness to trust the instincts of the actors. Wendy Robie, who played the eyepatch-wearing Nadine Hurley, recalls that during the episode, Nadine walks in on her husband, Big Ed (Everett McGill), and Norma Jennings (Peggy Lipton) in bed together and proceeds to lie down with them and detail the events of her day. It's an awkward and genuinely funny moment. The script called for Nadine, full of super-strength, to remove the door from its hinges when she entered the room. During one of the multiple takes, the actor injured her leg tearing off the door. As a result, Keaton suggested Robie choose the take she liked best, as recompense for being "wounded in service." Willing to suffer for her own art, and impressed that she hadn't flinched when door met flesh, Robie chose the take in which she was injured.

Director Tim Hunter, a fellow student alongside David Lynch at the American Film Institute Cultural Centre who had previously made a name for himself with 1986's *River's Edge*, worked on multiple *Twin Peaks* episodes, including "Arbitrary Law" (2.09), which featured Leland Palmer's death in a Twin Peaks jail cell. It's a powerful, fitting send-off for the series lead that features obtuse angles and tight tracking shots leading up to the moment, followed by a series of intimate close-ups with minimal cuts that places an emphasis on faces: Leland's as he delivers an emotional confession and Cooper's as he guides Leland into the next world. While not necessarily "consciously arty," as Hunter described the series as a whole in 2012, the scene remains a classic moment.

In 2015, it's easy to take auteur television for granted. Both network and cable channels are full of high-quality series, striving and oftentimes succeeding at making work as groundbreaking and creative as the most critically acclaimed films. Not only are audiences willing to be challenged and impressed, many of them demand it. But back in 1990, David Lynch's willingness to push the boundaries of network television as far as they could go made *Twin Peaks* the first to bring the style and approach of art house cinema into the living rooms of North America.

3

"A different set of blueprints"

One of the hallmarks of *Twin Peaks* is the simple fact that a viewer never knows what to expect. The show dominated water-cooler talk during its initial run because its stories and characters left much open to interpretation, discussion, and dissection. Beyond the catchphrase mysteries — "Who killed Laura Palmer?" "Who shot Agent Cooper?" — were the deeper queries. What is the Black Lodge? Why is Leland always crying? What do the dreams mean and are they reliable? Unlike the other popular nighttime dramas of the era, nothing was ever as it seemed in the world of *Twin Peaks*.

Soap operas — whether nighttime dramas or daytime stories — rely heavily on a host of storytelling conventions that viewers are familiar with and have come to expect, from the evil twin to the cheating husband to the family feud. In the '80s,

Dynasty, Dallas, Knots Landing, and *Falcon Crest* nabbed great ratings by trading in those clichés, with episodes often ending in a cliffhanger. *Dallas* really defined the use of cliffhanger finales, with 1980's shooting of J.R. Ewing. That monumental television event begat the "Who shot J.R.?" pop culture phenomenon, echoed a decade later by *Twin Peaks*. Such formulaic fare entertains, delivering ratings without making audiences think too hard. (And hey, I grew up loving *Dallas*.)

In fact, as renowned as it is as an influential cult classic, *Twin Peaks* has much in common with its soapy precursors. Everywhere you look, you find teenage love affairs, philandering husbands and wives, mystery, intrigue, and mistaken identity in a town full of good-looking people. The first season finale pulled out all the usual stops: a fire, attempted suicide, multiple assaults and shootings, even murder. You'd be hard pressed to find an episode of any series riddled with more tropes. David Lynch and Mark Frost were well aware that they were playing in the soap opera sandbox, but their ambition for *Twin Peaks* ensured that it transcended and redefined the genre. "I thought of [*Twin Peaks*] as subversive and radical," recalled Mark Frost. "I was trying to subvert the whole format of the nighttime soap. We were trying to undermine the falsities that those things relied upon, melodrama and ridiculous emotional scenes. They didn't get to the truth of anything."[26]

Undermining false emotion and uncovering the unusual, the darkness that lay underneath the veneer of normalcy, was an obsession in Lynch's cinematic work and became, in many ways, *Twin Peaks'* raison d'être. This is evident in the complex characters who can't be pigeonholed. Benjamin Horne is not simply the town's slimy rich resident, hungry for power and lustful for women; as the series progresses, he develops into a wounded man who strives to find goodness. Unlike other soap-opera templates, Ben doesn't fall back into the same rut (womanize/repent/womanize, scheme/fail/scheme again) — instead, he falls (by losing his Ghostwood Estates deal amid accusations that he killed Laura Palmer), climbs back up, and looks for redemption, which he almost finds (with his new-found environmentalist ways, his daughter beside him). The way he gets there is characteristically funny and strange: on what other show do psychological breakthroughs happen during Civil War reenactments? Where the first season and a good portion of the second position Ben as the baddest man in town, the character spends the later half of the series attempting to make up for past transgressions, such as an affair with Eileen Hayward that led to the birth of Donna. He is determined to "do good" and build a relationship with Donna — although of course redemption doesn't come easy, and his attempts at reconciliation may have cost him his life. A cliff-hanger that may be resolved when *Twin Peaks* returns in 2016.

Even the more offbeat and unusual characters we meet have real pathos to them. The Log Lady (Catherine Coulson), who carries a log that "talks" to her wherever she goes, is one of the show's most defining characters. But the Log Lady isn't simply played as an oddity or for laughs (though she does inspire a few, such as the moment in the pilot where she vigorously turns the lights on and off as Agent Cooper waits to address the townspeople). Her backstory, revealed in "Cooper's Dreams" (1.06), is actually quite tragic — her husband, a woodsman, died in a fire the day after their wedding. Another strange character, the eyepatch-wearing, super-strong Nadine Hurley is also a tragic figure; the crazed, domineering wife of Big Ed was actually a wallflower who lost her eye in a hunting accident while the two were on their honeymoon. There's a real depth to Nadine once we scratch beneath the surface, certainly more so than other supporting characters on nighttime soap operas.

But there's little depth to be found in *Invitation to Love*, the Mark Frost–directed show-within-a-show often seen on the townspeople's television screens during the first season of *Twin Peaks*. Its over-the-top metafictional soap opera moments usually mimic what is transpiring on *Twin Peaks*. The arrival of Laura Palmer's lookalike cousin in "Rest in Pain" (1.04) is mirrored on *Invitation to Love* with identical twins (complete with matching soap names), Jade and Emerald. Though they look the same, Jade and Emerald are opposites, just as Madeleine and Laura are. When Leo Johnson (Eric DaRe) is shot by Hank Jennings (Chris Mulkey) in the season one finale, "The Last Evening" (1.08), *Invitation to Love* is on the TV set in the room, the scene showing Montana being gunned down.

From the overwrought dialogue to the clichéd costuming, *Invitation to Love* openly mocks the genre Frost and Lynch were redefining. There's a wink and a nod to the audience whenever it appears; *Twin Peaks'* writers know the genre they're toying with. *Invitation to Love* is heavy with expected exaggeration, whereas *Twin Peaks* explores emotions in a far more interesting manner. For this viewer, *Invitation to Love* never particularly worked, not upon first viewing and even less so after subsequent ones. More often than not, it just seems forced, a bit of a misstep that interrupts the flow of any given episode. Perhaps the creators wound up feeling the same way — *Invitation to Love* wasn't invited back to the second season of *Twin Peaks*.

At the heart of both daytime and nighttime soap operas (and even show-within-a-show soaps like *Invitation to Love*) is intense emotion, and as part of Lynch and Frost's playfulness with the genre, exaggerated emotion became part of *Twin Peaks'* modus operandi. Characters don't just enjoy a meal; they overindulge in orgasmic, and oftentimes hilarious, intakes of coffee and food. "I plan on writing an epic poem about this gorgeous pie," says FBI Regional Bureau Chief Gordon Cole (David Lynch) upon eating a slice at the Double R Diner in "On the Wings of Love" (2.18). Nor do they simply cry or grieve: characters weep and wail as sorrow tears at their souls. Sometimes this is done with a sense of humor, such as with the character of Andy Brennan (Harry Goaz), a deputy in the Twin Peaks Sheriff's Department with a tendency to cry at the most inopportune occasions. In the pilot, he bursts into tears while photographing Laura Palmer's body, still wrapped in plastic. "Is this going to happen every damn time?" Sheriff Truman questions his deputy, that one sentence giving us a real insight into Andy's sweet, bumbling nature. It's a moment of levity in a serious situation and is amusingly par for the course with this character. Later in that same episode, Andy is seen weeping again upon the discovery of the murder site. "Tell Harry I didn't cry," he says over the walkie-talkie to Lucy.

Leland Palmer is also a serial crier, but his tears have a very different effect. We meet Leland in the first hour of the *Twin Peaks* pilot: he's working at the Great Northern Hotel as lawyer to the town's wealthiest citizen, Benjamin Horne. When Leland's wife, Sarah, calls concerned about Laura, he is supportive and reassuring, the perfect husband and father. But, in one of the most emotional moments of the episode, Leland is visibly crushed the moment he sees Sheriff Truman arrive: Leland knows that something horrible has happened to Laura. Truman never actually has to utter the words. Instead, Leland drops the phone in his hand, Sarah's voice pleading for information. When Ben Horne comes out of a meeting and asks what's wrong, Leland says through his tears, "My daughter's dead."

For the duration of season one, Leland is a bereaved father, unable to contain the myriad emotions he is dealing with. The clichéd, emotionally overwrought soap-opera convention is reimagined here: Ray Wise's performance is extreme and yet believably earnest. At one moment he is quiet, almost introspective, struggling to maintain his composure. At the next he is the quintessential dancing fool, spurred to movement at the drop of a needle. This transformation occurs multiple times throughout season one — during "Zen, or the Skill to Catch a Killer" (1.03), when Leland maniacally dances around the Palmer living room with a portrait of Laura in his arms, a scene played for heartbreak and horror; in "Rest in Pain" (1.04), standing by himself on the dance floor of the Great Northern Hotel, begging any of the gathered townspeople to dance with him; in "Cooper's Dreams" (1.06), during a business meeting with potential new investors for Benjamin Horne's Ghostwood Estates project. This instance, different than previous ones, is played for laughs, as Leland's sudden crazed dancing leads others, including Catherine Martell (Piper Laurie) and Jerry Horne, to join him on the dance floor, where they all "do the Leland." Watching Benjamin Horne squirm as his once-trusted lawyer has another breakdown is definitely amusing, but when the camera focuses in on a weeping Audrey Horne (Sherilyn Fenn) seeing all this transpire, we're reminded that the psychological upheaval Leland is suffering shouldn't actually be funny. Has any television character been put through the emotional wringer as much as Leland Palmer? His extreme emotion hits a crescendo when, in "Rest in Pain" (1.04), Leland pitches himself onto his daughter's casket as it's being lowered into the ground. In this moment, we're provoked into two dueling reactions — laughter at the absurdity, and sadness at the grief-stricken father of a murdered girl. Take your pick, because neither one is wrong.

Leland reaches catharsis in "The Last Evening" (1.08), the season one finale, by killing a prime suspect in Laura's murder, Jacques Renault (Walter Olkewicz). Season two sees a drastic change in Leland's appearance and manner: his hair has turned snow white, a smile never leaves his face, and all of his grief has seemingly dissipated. It appears that Leland Palmer is ready to get back to life in Twin Peaks once again. However, these radical changes foreshadow the character's connection to BOB, his other self.

Whereas the Leland Palmer of season one is a study in exaggerated grief, season two's Leland is a caricature of happiness, taken to the extreme. In "May the Giant Be With You" (2.01), he croons "Mairzy Doats" over and over, shocking his wife and niece in a surreal moment of insanity that only David Lynch could deliver. Amazingly, it's topped minutes later when Leland arrives at the Great Northern Hotel and walks into Benjamin Horne's office, still singing that same song. Instead of reacting with trepidation as Sarah and Maddy do, Benjamin and his brother, Jerry, embrace the absurdity and begin dancing themselves, Jerry doing the worm in the middle of the office while Ben does a tap-shoe routine on top of his desk. It's a classic *Twin Peaks* moment — at once hilarious, disturbing, and unprecedented. Thanks to the nonplussed reaction of the Hornes, the audience is left wondering if everyone in Twin Peaks is unstable in their own special way, each one capable of great lightness or horrific darkness.

While many popular shows — *Hill Street Blues*; *Magnum, P.I.*; *Simon & Simon*; *Remington Steele*; and *Murder, She Wrote*, to name just a few — had mysteries and murder at their cores, few (if any) structured a season-long arc around a central mystery. (*Dallas* revealed who shot J.R. just four episodes into its fourth season.) One show the creators of *Twin Peaks* cite as an inspiration for their style of serial storytelling is CBS's *The Fugitive*, which, for four seasons between 1963 and 1967, chronicled escaped convict Dr. Richard Kimble's pursuit of the One-Armed Man he alleged had killed his wife. But while *Twin Peaks* even had its own One-Armed Man, traveling shoe salesman Philip Gerard (named after the police lieutenant pursuing Kimble), the key difference with *The Fugitive* is that it's a tale of chase above mystery. The thrill and enjoyment of the show is not in deducing, but in Kimble's elusion of law enforcement and pursuit of the One-Armed Man. *Twin Peaks* has an ever-expanding mystery at its core, one that, unbeknownst to its initial rabid audience, the creators were in no hurry to resolve. Lynch and Frost's plan to have Laura's murder fade into the background as viewers became more engaged with the living citizens of Twin Peaks was at odds with the whodunit-focused marketing of the first season and with the genre expectations that viewers — however initially willing to go on the strange journey with Lynch and Frost — still maintained. Ambitious as the creators' plan was, the rank-and-file *Twin Peaks* audience was prepared to wait only so long for satisfaction; the increasing lack of closure contributed to the significant decline in ratings early on in its second season.

Twin Peaks didn't immediately redefine the nighttime soap opera. Far from it, in fact, as a few months after its premiere, *Beverly Hills, 90210* began its decade-long run on the FOX network, followed in 1992 by its spinoff, *Melrose Place*. What *Twin Peaks* did ultimately do, however, was model the unexplored possibilities that the medium held. It would just take a few years before other TV show creators revisited that strange terrain.

4

"One . . . and the same"

In "Beyond Life and Death" (2.22), the heroic Special Agent Dale Cooper is in pursuit of his new love, Annie Blackburn (Heather Graham), who has entered the Black Lodge as the prisoner of Windom Earle (Kenneth Welsh). Though Cooper has glimpsed the Lodge and encountered its inhabitants in his dreams, this is the first time he physically ventures in. We once again see the familiar elements of this supernatural meeting space — the blood-red curtains and zigzagged floors — but what was originally a strange set piece is now something far more sinister and evil. A lonesome jazz singer croons about walking through the sycamore trees; strobe lights flash, disorienting both Cooper and the viewer. Cooper walks the hypnotic halls, each room mirroring the next, and he is confronted by the Black Lodge's denizens and guests — BOB, the

Man from Another Place, Windom Earle, twisted versions of Laura and Leland Palmer, and — finally — himself. In the end, Cooper emerges from the Black Lodge possessed by BOB, with the "good Dale" (as Annie Blackburn refers to him in *Fire Walk with Me*) trapped in the Lodge.

Cue the credits.

The final, frightening hour of *Twin Peaks* enveloped audiences in a hypnotic, dreamlike world — entrancing, confusing, and denying expectations by leaving much unresolved — and left the hero of the story with a split identity, his darkness in control, at least for now.

While contemporary television has a rather high population of doppelgängers, clones, alt-world selves, and evil twins, the storytelling device was once more common to literature than TV. A doppelgänger (*doppel* meaning double, and *gänger*, walker) is the paranormal or sinister double of someone or something, or a person psychologically split in two. Doubles have long made for popular storytelling, allowing an audience to gain a greater understanding of a character — two opposing sides of a whole explored in depth. More often than not, the doppelgänger or double allows for exploration of human nature, the shades between good and evil, conflicting impulses and traits, right and wrong. In response to being outed as his pseudonym, Richard Bachman, a more violent, less stylized writer than himself, Stephen King responded by crafting 1989's *The Dark Half*, in which the protagonist, Thad Beaumont, a writer himself, is stalked by his own, more successful pseudonym, George Stark, who has seemingly come to life and embarked upon a killing spree in response to being "killed off" by his creator. Robert Louis Stevenson's 1886 novella *The Strange Case of Dr. Jekyll and Mr. Hyde* is perhaps the most enduring and well known of the doppel-gänger stories. The good Dr. Henry Jekyll unleashes the violent Edward Hyde inside him, battling for control of himself before ultimately losing to Hyde, the more "genuine man" of the two. Film is no stranger to doubles either: classics include Alfred Hitchcock's *Vertigo* (1958) and more recently Darren Aronofsky's *Black Swan* (2010). I'd be remiss if I didn't also mention David Lynch's own cinematic doppelgänger extrava-ganza, 1997's *Lost Highway*. Bill Pullman portrays saxophonist Fred Madison who, upon being placed in jail and sentenced to death for murdering his wife (Patricia Arquette), morphs into an entirely different, younger person (played by Balthazar Getty). He begins an affair with a client's wife, who is the spit-ting image of his own dead wife. Like most Lynch films, *Lost Highway* is oftentimes inexplicable, though entertainingly so.

From the twin peaks of the town's name to the compli-cated portrait of Laura Palmer that is sketched in the series' first episodes, doubles and doppelgängers are a core concern of *Twin Peaks*, a foundation of its hallmark disquietude and allure. Beautiful, popular Laura is, at first blush, the idealized American teenager. She dates the quarterback of the football team and is the homecoming queen; she volunteers for Meals on Wheels, gives English lessons to Josie Packard, and tutors Johnny Horne (Robert Bauer), who "is 27 and is in the third grade; he's got emotional problems," according to his sister,

Audrey, in "Traces to Nowhere" (1.02). (To this day, I find myself wondering how Laura had time to take part in half the extracurricular activities she did *and* lead a dark secret life.)

A de facto Dr. Jekyll — a well-adjusted and meaningful member of her community, at ease with her role in the world — Laura is so beloved that Principal Wolchezk (Troy Evans) breaks down in grief when announcing her death to his students. How could something so horrible happen to someone so wonderful? As Cooper's investigation scratches beneath the perfect exterior, Laura's Mr. Hyde is not long to reveal itself: why does Laura have $10,000 in a safety deposit box, alongside a small bag containing traces of cocaine? Her secret affair with James Hurley, her strange relationship with psychiatrist Dr. Jacoby (Russ Tamblyn) — how did she keep this secret life hidden?

While we get glimpses of Laura's secret life through the parallel investigations that law enforcement and her friends conduct, it was not until Lynch's prequel film, *Twin Peaks: Fire Walk with Me*, that audiences saw the final seven days of Laura's life. She snorts cocaine in the bathroom stall at her high school. She drinks alone when her parents aren't at home. She has rough sex with multiple partners. All the while, she struggles to retain some facade of purity, but the "good girl" can't help but give way to the demon inside. It makes a sad sense that the series' and film's actual demon, BOB, lusts for Laura, both mentally and physically. As he says to her in *Fire Walk with Me*, "I want to taste through your mouth"; BOB sees a kindred spirit in the dark side of Laura. Her ability

43

to manipulate the people around her — Bobby Briggs, shut-in Harold Smith (Lenny von Dohlen), James Hurley — mirrors the control BOB has over his own victims.

The depth of Laura's character, and the struggle between her surface persona and what lay beneath, was first explored in depth when David Lynch's daughter Jennifer wrote *The Secret Diary of Laura Palmer* (1990), a *New York Times* bestseller released between the first and second seasons of *Twin Peaks*. At just 22 years old, Jennifer Lynch proved remarkably adept at getting into the head of 16-year-old Laura Palmer. As Jennifer recalled, "My father called me, I guess it was a few months into the first season, and he said, 'Jen-o, do you remember that day I picked you up from school and you told me that you were thinking about finding another girl's diary?' And I said, 'Yes, I'm surprised you remember that.' He said, 'Well, it stuck with me. Tell me about that again.' And I said I figured if I could find this diary, just tuck it under my jacket and get home with it, I could find out whether or not she feared or yearned for the same things I did. If I was good or bad based on some of the feelings I was having, about others, about myself, about my own body, etc., etc. He said, 'I would like to know if you would like to write Laura Palmer's diary.' And I said, 'Fuck, yeah!' So I guess it was about a week later that I went in and met with him and Mark, and that was when they closed the door and told me who killed Laura. They said, 'You know who she deals with. You know who's done it, you go ahead and you write whatever you think is best,' and I was given really total freedom."[27]

Jennifer Lynch's book traces Laura's life from her

44

adolescence and sexual awakening to her drug-fueled teenage life and abuse at the hands of BOB; its exploration of the two warring sides of the character's personality was an extremely useful resource for Sheryl Lee. "Part of my education as an actor was to write bios for my characters," remembers Lee. "Of course, I didn't write anything as eloquent as Jennifer did. But just the little notes I had taken about who Laura was before I played her, it was so synchronous. I hadn't told anybody. I felt like Jennifer was in my head, meaning Laura's head. And I always feel this intimate connection with Jennifer because of that. There's something there that connects us, having experienced that character that way."[28] Laura's secret diary would become pivotal during the early half of season two as Donna, James, and Maddy seek to recover it from Harold Smith, a shut-in who Laura knew from her Meals on Wheels deliveries. This is a rare case of dramatic irony on *Twin Peaks*, since many viewers had already seen inside the pages of the diary and had "insider" knowledge of Laura.

Beyond Laura's double life of good girl and deviant, the doppelgänger trope was explored more extensively in flesh-and-blood form: in "Rest in Pain" (1.04), Madeleine Ferguson arrives in Twin Peaks (from Missoula, MI, David Lynch's birthplace) to comfort her Aunt Sarah and Uncle Leland. Slightly older with darker hair and glasses, Maddy (also played by Sheryl Lee) is the spitting image of Laura. As she tells James of Laura, "We used to pretend we were sisters." In many ways, Maddy acts as a stand-in for Laura, in her role in the Palmer household — her comfortable silence with her

aunt and uncle allows us to see the family in better times —
and in her friendship with James and Donna. While she does
impersonate Laura over the phone, on video, and in person
(to enable James and Donna to investigate Dr. Jacoby), Maddy
comes to resemble Laura in what feels like an inevitable evo-
lution: from her literal appearance (she wears her glasses less
and less), to the horrors that haunt her (visions of violence
in domestic settings — of blood and BOB) and her romantic
choices (she and James kiss). And ultimately, her tragic fate
mirrors her cousin's: with Maddy's murder, the audience is
given a glimpse of Laura's own horrific final moments.

In that episode, "Lonely Souls" (2.07), the darkness in
Leland Palmer is revealed: he stares into a mirror and the face
of BOB looks back at him. While season one's Leland was a
man in extreme grief, his personality flips (and his hair color
changes) after the catharsis of murdering Jacques Renault.
The singing, dancing, and apparently carefree Leland we see
in season two is completely different; he's unhinged, but in a
functional manner now. It's as though he's dropped the bag-
gage he'd been carrying since Laura's death. The truth, when
revealed, was something genuinely shocking. Leland has been
and is possessed by BOB; he is his daughter's killer and abuser,
his white hair a physical manifestation of his possession. As
he murders Maddy, Laura's doppelgänger, the scene shifts
between the Jekyll-and-Hyde figures of Leland and BOB
committing the atrocity (an effect repeated in *Twin Peaks: Fire
Walk with Me*, when we witness Laura's murder) — they're one
and the same, two sides of the same coin.

Don't look for early clues to this revelation, though, in Ray Wise's magnificent performance as Leland Palmer: the actor didn't know his character was Laura's murderer. Leland's revelation in "Coma" (2.02) that he knew BOB as a child, as his grandfather's summer cottage neighbor, wound up being a red herring for both the audience and the actor, who didn't discover the truth until it came time to shoot "Lonely Souls" (2.07). "I certainly knew that I was one of many who could have possibly done it," recalls Wise. "And I certainly didn't want it to be me. Number one, I didn't want to leave town, and number two, the thought of being the killer of my own daughter was anathema to me. It was the most terrible thought that I could conjure up in my brain. I was hoping and praying it wasn't me."[29]

During Leland Palmer's final moments, Ray Wise once more conveys the dual sides of the character — one possessed by the evil sprit that haunts the woods of Twin Peaks, devoid of sympathy for the souls he destroys and lives he takes; the other, a good man, the grieving father, realizing on his deathbed that he's unwittingly committed horrible sins.

Nothing is as it seems in *Twin Peaks*, and the secrets harbored by its citizens challenge viewers' initial expectations of the characters. Laura Palmer's boyfriend, Bobby, and his best friend, Mike (Gary Hershberger), are high school jocks who sneer at authority, at first glance stock characters we've seen before. Bobby, in particular, becomes more layered as the series progresses: not only does he have a secret girlfriend, but he deals cocaine, caught up with the town's criminal underbelly.

His outburst at Laura's funeral, where he admonishes those gathered for not helping her when they had the chance, is more thoughtful than one would expect from the character, as are the tears he sheds during that emotional encounter with his father in "May the Giant Be with You" (2.01). From the series' beginning, the two are at odds: in "Traces to Nowhere" (1.02), Major Briggs parents with a stiff upper lip, speaking to Bobby with little emotion, as if he is one of his soldiers. Major Briggs cannot tolerate disrespect, going so far as to slap a cigarette from Bobby's mouth when the boy lights up at the dinner table. Father and son finally connect, in a powerful moment at the Double R Diner. In a speech lasting an unusual three minutes, Major Briggs recounts a stirring vision of Bobby he had the night before ("as distinguished from a dream, which is a mere sorting and cataloging of the day's events by the subconscious," explains the Major); in his vision, Major Briggs is at his childhood home, where he encounters Bobby, "happy and carefree, clearly living a life of deep harmony and joy." As the Major speaks, tears form in Bobby's eyes, and we see there's soul underneath his gruff, disrespectful exterior. "I awoke with a tremendous feeling of optimism and confidence in you and your future," Major Briggs concludes. Bobby is in awe that his father has genuine hope for him despite how strained their father-son relationship has been. (Throughout the second season of *Twin Peaks*, bad-boy Bobby loses his edge, becoming less of a badass, a change that didn't sit well with actor Dana Ashbrook — "I wasn't too crazy about the fact they were softening me up so much," he recalls.[30])

Josie Packard begins the series as a seemingly ill-at-ease widow, fearful that her sister-in-law, Catherine Martell, and Ben Horne are out to destroy her. She first appears soft and sweet, but by the time of her death in "The Condemned Woman" (2.16), we've learned that Josie has conspired to murder while killing others herself. In fact, she was the one who pulled the trigger on Agent Cooper at the end of "The Last Evening" (1.08); she is the show's real femme fatale. Certainly more so than Audrey Horne, who is presented as an ingénue with enticing sexuality throughout season one. However, when her affair with John Justice Wheeler (Billy Zane) culminates in "The Path to the Black Lodge" (2.20), it's revealed that she is a virgin.

The bit players throughout the series even have complex dual sides — some, like David Duchovny's cross-dressing FBI agent, Denise/Dennis Bryson, are obvious and used for good humor; Denise's arrival — and her flirting with Sheriff Truman — in "Masked Ball" (2.11) is a second-season high point. Others come out over the course of a few episodes, such as the subplot revelation that Norma Jennings's mother (Jane Greer), who arrives in town with her new husband in "Drive with a Dead Girl" (2.08), is also M.T. Wentz, a mean-spirited food critic who gives her own daughter's restaurant a horrible review.

Wearing a uniform of dark suit, tie, and trench coat, armed with a cup of coffee in one hand and a Dictaphone in the other, Dale Cooper is the definitive face of goodness on *Twin Peaks*. David Lynch, who named the character after D.B. Cooper, the name given by the media to the unidentified man who hijacked a Boeing 727 in 1971, helped make Agent Cooper so distinctive a character with his various Lynchisms, like Cooper's spirituality and his dictated notes to Diane. Some critics and fans have theorized that MacLachlan serves as Lynch's stand-in, both in *Twin Peaks* and in the Lynch films in which MacLachlan appears, and while Lynch has always been forthright about his connection to Cooper, Mark Frost also had his hand in shaping the character, adding Sherlockian touches, for example. One of the most poignant moments in the series comes courtesy of Mark Frost when, in the final moments of his life, Leland Palmer faces the horrors he has committed and begs for forgiveness. With Leland's head in Cooper's lap, water pouring from the sprinkler system in the Sheriff's Department's jail cell, it is the mystic side of Dale Cooper that helps guide Leland through his death, with words written from the pen of Mark Frost as inspired by the Tibetan Book of the Dead. "The time has come for you to seek the Path," says Cooper. "Your soul has set you face to face before the clear light . . . and now you are about to experience it in its reality, wherein all things are like the void and cloudless sky, and the naked, spotless intellect is like a transparent vacuum, without circumference or center . . . At this moment, know yourself and abide in that state. Look to the light, Leland. Find the light."

Herein lies an incredible piece of Cooper's complexity. The character has come to town to solve the murder of a teenage girl, and has faced his own mortality in his search for the truth. Upon discovering the culprit, Cooper plays both lawman and spiritual guide. Cooper sees the world of Twin Peaks — and we see our world reflected therein — for what it truly is: a place that doesn't exist in black and white, but in a multitude of grays.

Though painted as a white knight when he first meets Audrey, Benjamin Horne's daughter, who has a way with a cherry stem, Cooper is clearly struck by this teenage girl. In "Traces to Nowhere" (1.02), Coop first lays eyes on her, in the dining room of the Great Northern Hotel, as he is finishing his order for grapefruit juice — "just as long as those grapefruits are . . . freshly squeezed." The innuendo of the moment is loud and clear, and while the scene between them is friendly and cordial on Cooper's end, as he questions Audrey about her relationship with Laura Palmer, Audrey is more interested in asking some suggestive questions: "Do you like my ring? . . . Sometimes I get so flushed. . . . Do your palms ever itch?" While the show certainly plays up Audrey's sexuality in this first scene, one would still expect Cooper to be able to play it cool around her. Instead, when she walks into his gaze that morning at the Great Northern Hotel, a sexual side of the special agent manifests itself, though Cooper buries it amidst his FBI protocol.

As the season progresses, the duo establish a questionable friendship. Audrey is smitten with the dashing agent; she wants to assist him in his investigation to be close to him. Cooper elects to establish boundaries, though there are moments of reluctance, even hints of lasciviousness. In "Cooper's Dreams" (1.06), there is a definite intonation in Cooper's voice that's a little more than cordial.

COOPER
Audrey, you'll have to excuse me this morning.
I'm running late. I only have time for coffee.

AUDREY
Well, maybe I could go with you.

COOPER
Wednesdays were traditionally a school
day when I was your age.

AUDREY
(leaning in)
I can't believe you were ever my age.

COOPER
I've got the pictures to prove it.
[pauses] How old are you?

AUDREY
Eighteen.

COOPER
See you later, Audrey.

A young, beautiful girl. An older man in power. So much of *Twin Peaks* is built upon these roles — Benjamin Horne and the women he employs at One Eyed Jacks; Leland Palmer and Teresa Banks (Pamela Gidley); BOB/Leland and Laura; the abusive trucker Leo Johnson and his young waitress wife, Shelly (Mädchen Amick). Cooper could have been one of them, had he succumbed to the temptation, but instead, he is vigilant, battling with himself to dampen his desire for Audrey. Even when she shows up naked in his hotel room in "Realization Time" (1.07), begging him not to make her leave.

COOPER

What I want and what I need are two different things,
Audrey. When a man joins the Bureau he takes an oath
to uphold certain values. Values that he's sworn to live by.
This is wrong, Audrey; we both know it.

AUDREY

But don't you like me?

COOPER

I like you very much. You're beautiful, intelligent,
desirable. You're everything a man wants in his life.
But what you need right now, more than anything else,
is a friend. Someone who will listen.

It's important to note that the original plan for the Audrey-Cooper relationship was for it to become the focus of the second season, as the search for Laura Palmer's killer went on the back burner. However, Kyle MacLachlan reportedly put a stop to it (allegedly at the behest of his then-girlfriend Lara

Flynn Boyle, *Twin Peaks'* Donna Hayward), suggesting to the producers that Cooper was not the type of man to enter into a relationship with a teenage girl. While it may be an interesting bit of *Twin Peaks* making-of history, these early plans also give an indication that the writers and producers viewed Cooper as morally ambiguous. In season two, Cooper winds up developing a new relationship, with Annie Blackburn, fresh out of a convent and not much older than Audrey herself. It's through Cooper's blossoming relationship with Annie that we discover just how flawed our heroic lead actually is, when Cooper reveals to her that the last person he truly loved was a married woman — Caroline Earle, wife of Cooper's mentor and original FBI partner, Windom Earle.

Though he initially appears to be on the straight and narrow, Agent Cooper is far from a by-the-book lawman. Cooper is driven by an inherent sense of right and wrong, rule book be damned. While his investigative style may be eclectic and unusual, his motivation emanates from the character's desire to do good. Cooper uses traditional police methods of detection to try to uncover Laura Palmer's murder, but also throws rocks at bottles to determine a prime suspect. Though he professes his desire to uphold the values of the FBI, he has no problem breaking international law when he travels to Canada with the Bookhouse Boys. He'll rebuff the advances of a teenage girl, but then admit to committing adultery and betraying the trust of his partner and friend.

Windom Earle is Cooper gone bad, an evil double that may or may not have been unleashed when his wife had an affair with Cooper, and it's Dale's responsibility to find and capture him. As the main villain for the second half of season two and Cooper's evil opposite, Earle is presented as having no redeeming qualities (allowing the great Kenneth Welsh to go to crazy town in his portrayal). While both characters are interested in Tibet and the mystical, Earle partakes in black magic while Cooper clearly embraces the light. Even with the mistakes he makes and risks he takes, Cooper is inherently a good man, while Earle murders indiscriminately in his quest to both kill Cooper and gain entrance into the Black Lodge. In Earle, Cooper (and the audience) sees what could happen should he stray from the path of righteousness.

During the final hour of *Twin Peaks*, Special Agent Dale Cooper enters the Black Lodge of his own volition, in pursuit of Earle and Annie. Inside, he is haunted by doppelgängers of Leland and Laura Palmer, eyeing him with unhinged malice as they comb the confusing hallways. He encounters the soul of Caroline Earle, his one-time lover, killed at the hands of her deranged husband, and comes face to face with BOB. Finally, Cooper flees from a maniacal doppelgänger of himself, his inner darkness made manifest. Ultimately, Cooper, the white knight who arrived in Twin Peaks to do good, doesn't prove strong enough to resist the darkness that resides inside the Black Lodge.

With that, *Twin Peaks* was over, but that didn't mean Cooper's story had concluded in the head of his creators. "People were really upset that it ended with an evil Cooper who'd been taken over by BOB," said David Lynch. "But that's *not* the ending. That's the ending that people were stuck with. That's just the ending of the second season. If it had continued . . ."³¹

In the world of *Twin Peaks*, it's not only characters who are doppelgänged, but also the locations and occupations (and even the accounting ledgers). Throughout the series, earnest Sheriff's secretary Lucy Moran, Deputy Hawk (Michael Horse), and the dim but dutiful Deputy Andy Brennan have an unwavering devotion to justice and to their boss, Sheriff Harry S. Truman, himself an honorable lawman through and through, and are willing to work with Agent Cooper to solve Laura's murder. However, in the prequel film *Twin Peaks: Fire Walk with Me*, FBI Agents Chet Desmond (Chris Isaak) and Sam Stanley (Kiefer Sutherland) encounter the local law enforcement of Deer Meadow while investigating the murder of BOB/Leland's first victim, Teresa Banks, a police department that is the mirror opposite. Unlike the warm and exceedingly helpful members of the Twin Peaks Sheriff's Department that Agent Cooper (and the audience) grow to love, the Deer Meadow PD are obnoxious, boorish, defensive, and unhelpful. In the much-sought-after deleted scenes of the film, Agent Desmond actually comes to blows with Deer Meadow's Sheriff Cable (Gary Bullock). After he and Stanley examine the body of Teresa Banks, they stop off for, what else, a late night cup of coffee at the lesser counterpart to Twin Peaks' Double R Diner. The scene at Hap's Diner takes place in the dead of night (roughly 3 a.m.) with flickering lights and few customers, a contrast to most of the brightly lit scenes at the

Double R. The waitress, Irene (Sandra Kinder), is older and a little worse for wear than former Miss Twin Peaks Norma Jennings, who always has a kind word. "You want to hear our specials?" asks Irene. "We don't have any."

Counterparts abound throughout the series, whether as doppelgängers, doubles, mirror images, or, as Deputy Hawk mentions in "Masked Ball" (2.11), shadow selves. The homey Double R finds counterparts in both Hap's Diner and the Roadhouse, a bar full of violence and haunting revelations. The perfume counter at Horne's Department Store is where One Eyed Jacks, the casino and brothel also owned by Benjamin Horne, finds young women to work as prostitutes north of the border. Even the role of protecting the citizens of Twin Peaks is split: there is the public face of the law with the Sheriff's Department, and then there are the Bookhouse Boys, a clandestine group that operates undercover in instances that can't be handled by the book, as it were. (Of course, the secret society members include Sheriff Truman, Deputy Hawk, and, after his initiation, Agent Cooper himself — working both by the letter of the law and outside of it.) Finally, the sense of wholesome and familiar small-town America is starkly contrasted by the Black Lodge, the extra-dimensional supernatural meeting place for evil that manifests itself in the form of BOB. While the theoretical opposite of the Black Lodge may be the White Lodge, referred to by Windom Earle in "Variations on Relations" (2.19), the characters never venture there during the series. (Perhaps the town is a corrupted version of the White Lodge?) Deciphering the meaning and significance of the Black Lodge was a huge part of fan conversation during the first season of the show. Peering beneath or through a facade of normalcy into a strange world that lies just beyond or beside it made *Twin Peaks*, like the rest of Lynch's work, surreal and ultimately without a firm or fixed singular meaning. While the lack of clear-cut explanations frustrated the more casual viewer, the fluidity and duality that extended from place to character resonated with many others, which lent a longevity to *Twin Peaks*' legacy and an often-imitated approach to storytelling.

Twin Peaks may be that weird show with the quirky characters, but it was also a program that delved into humanity's complexity, refusing to flinch or look away in our darkest moments. Lynch and Frost had left the '50s ideal far behind, but in showing their characters' struggles with the light and dark within, they offered a more realistic, and more interesting, portrait of goodness.

5

"What is going on in this house?"

Throw a rock in Twin Peaks and you'll hit familial dysfunction, some quite understated, some suitable for soap opera storylines. James Hurley lives with his uncle, Big Ed, because his mother is an alcoholic who disappears for weeks at a time. Norma Jennings has a tempestuous relationship with her mother at the best of times, a tension that is only exacerbated when she discovers that good ol' mom is more than she appears to be. Catherine Martell views her husband, Pete (Jack Nance), the sweetest man in town, with barely disguised contempt; she's equally cold to Josie Packard, the widow of her brother, with whom she and Pete share a home. *Twin Peaks* takes conventional family units and moments and blows them up to show the good and bad of it all.

When we first meet Benjamin Horne and his daughter,

there is little love between the two of them; after Audrey amusingly sabotages her father's business negotiations with a group of Norwegians, in "Traces to Nowhere" (1.02), he angrily tells her, "Laura died two days ago. I lost you years ago." It's a comment that later takes on a whole new level of dysfunction, when we discover that Ben had been carrying on an affair with Laura Palmer, a girl the same age as his own daughter. The Horne family drama continues with one of my favorite moments from the entire series, in "Zen, or the Skill to Catch a Killer" (1.03). Gathered around a giant dining room table for dinner, the Hornes sit in silence for an uncomfortably long time. It's quintessential David Lynch — the conventional family sit-down dinner twisted into something off-kilter — and goes against the primary instinct of network television: to fill silence. That silence is broken only when Ben's brother, Jerry, enters with brie and baguette sandwiches. Ben and Jerry dig into their sandwiches, cutting the tension of the scene and delivering a seriously funny moment — one of the bonds between brothers is their reverential devotion to the sublime pleasures of food. Following their chow-down, Ben decides to bolt with Jerry to One Eyed Jacks (another bonding experience for the brothers). Ben looks at his wife and children and, with a suitable amount of scorn, simply says, "Always a pleasure."

Benjamin Horne is a man of appearances — his family helps his legitimate business, and his anger at Audrey comes from her increasing refusal to play the well-behaved little daughter. Her disobedience manifests in an effort to help Cooper in his investigation, and her secret misbehavior leads her unwittingly to her father's favorite pastime. In "May the Giant Be With You" (2.01), Audrey has infiltrated the casino/brothel One Eyed Jacks, looking for clues to Laura Palmer's murder, and as the new girl, she's expected to show the owner a *very* good time.

Of course, the owner is her father.

Masked, Audrey squirms and (successfully) avoids the advances of Ben; it's disturbing and more than a little hard to watch. Ben's aggressive lasciviousness, though not quite violent, is frightening. The audience fears for Audrey and the scene takes on a tone of potential incest. Not only do we get a glimpse of the relationship between Ben and Laura Palmer (older, powerful man/younger, vulnerable woman), but this scene foreshadows in pantomime the shock of Leland as sexual aggressor to his own daughter, Laura.

Surprisingly, as the second season progresses, the relationship between the Horne father and daughter does an about face. During Ben's mental breakdown and his Civil War reenactments, it's Audrey who is constantly by his side, trying to help her father through his crazed circumstances. When he finally has his epiphany about becoming a good person, he seeks to find a spot in his family's life again. He apologizes to Audrey for being a distant father and sets about teaching her the family business (the lawful side of it, that is). In return, she forgives him for his multiple transgressions and joins him in his environmental causes, a decision that may or may not cost her her life in the series finale. (If there had been a third season, all involved have agreed that Audrey would have survived the explosion at the Twin Peaks Bank, where she had chained herself in an act of civil disobedience to save Ghostwood Forest). Ultimately, there is a positive resolution to Ben and Audrey's dynamic. Unlike the Laura and Leland relationship.

The Palmer family we meet in the pilot episode is broken by Laura's death. In one gloriously dark moment in "Zen, or the Skill to Catch a Killer" (1.03), a distraught Leland stands over the record player in his living room. He drops the needle and "Pennsylvania 6-5000" blares in all of its big-band glory. Leland picks up the framed photo of Laura as homecoming queen and with a low, bereaved moan that turns into a loud scream, he dances around the room, ever faster, until Sarah walks in and tries to grab the picture from him. The frame smashes against a table and breaks, bloodying Leland's hands. "What is going on in this house?" Sarah screams, as a tearful Leland wipes blood across the image of his dead daughter (an improvised moment after Ray Wise received a very real cut from the shattered glass). *The Brady Bunch* this is not: television grief had never been so strange, uncomfortable, or just plain weird. And we haven't even gotten to Laura Palmer's funeral.

The townspeople of Twin Peaks gather to pay respect to the dearly departed, and in what begins as a calm moment, Leland and Sarah stand stoically by Laura's grave, listening to the presiding priest (who tutored Laura in Sunday school) recite some words from the Bible and then recount his own relationship with the deceased. But the placid funeral scene crumbles, as Bobby Briggs berates those gathered for not helping Laura fight her demons and then proceeds to get into a fistfight with James Hurley, her secret boyfriend. As the crowd breaks them up, the camera focuses back onto a tearful Leland Palmer who, without warning, throws himself onto Laura's coffin, embracing it as it is being lowered into the ground. The Angelo Badalamenti score that plays during the moment is subtle and soft, suggesting that this is a tragic moment, and Sarah says to Leland with equal parts malice, heartache, and frustration, "Don't ruin this too."

This fan has always viewed this scene as yet another definitive *Twin Peaks* moment. Though the episode was deftly written by Harley Peyton and directed by Tina Rathbone, respectively, it's unquestionably filtered through a very Lynchian lens. It's a combination of black humor (the casket lowering device malfunctions with Leland on top of it and the camera lingers as it moves in and out of the shot) mixed with real tragedy (we are at the funeral for a murdered girl, after all). Back in November 1990, after the revelation that Leland killed Laura, *Chicago Tribune* writer M.C. Blakeman argued that the funeral scene was an early signal that Laura had been the victim of incest:

> One of the more obvious tipoffs about Leland's abuse came on the day of Laura's funeral. Flinging himself into the freshly dug grave, he sprawled on top of her coffin, riding it up and down again and again as the device that was supposed to have lowered Laura into the ground malfunctioned. Instead of going to her eternal rest, Laura Palmer was again violated in this deranged re-creation of sex in the "missionary position."[32]

In the same piece, Blakeman also singles out various clues throughout the series that point to the same assumption, some of which are certainly valid, while others, such as the one above, may be a little more open to interpretation.

Making Leland Palmer Laura's killer was a brave and bold decision for David Lynch and Mark Frost. Though Lynch had included allusions to incest in both *Blue Velvet* (1986) and *Wild at Heart* (1990), the subject of incest had never been dealt with on network television. The introduction of the taboo topic pushed the boundaries of what could be depicted on TV — couched though it was in the demonic BOB, whose possession of Leland was revealed to Cooper and Truman at the end of "Arbitrary Law" (2.09).

TRUMAN

I've lived in these woods all my life. I've heard some strange things. Seen some too. But this is way off the map. I'm having a hard time believing.

COOPER

Is it easier to believe a man would rape and murder his own daughter? Is that any more comforting?

TRUMAN

No.

The truth behind the horror that befell Laura Palmer was a shock to the characters, to the audience, and to the actors bringing *Twin Peaks* to life. "The revelation that it was her dad, I thought it was just a fucked-up thing," recalls Dana Ashbrook. "It made sense to me, all these crazy manifestations, all these things that came out."[33]

Not everyone associated with the show was satisfied with the explanation of Leland's possession by BOB, though. Jennifer Lynch, whose writing was fundamental in helping fully realize the character of Laura Palmer, recalls, "That was both the brilliance and my personal heartache about the series, that reaction, the excuse that he had to be possessed. For me, then it stops being about a father having sex with his child. And I'm not saying that there's not a level of hideous, dark possession and pain and evil that is in someone that does that. All I kept hearing is that BOB got into Leland, and it took the responsibility completely away from Leland. That I found really interesting. Nobody wanted to talk about it, which is why that interaction [between Cooper and Truman] was so potent. It clearly meant that mission on *Twin Peaks'* part was to say, 'We clearly know it's easier for you to hear it this.' It was certainly easier for ABC to screen it that way."[34]

When asked if she thought the character of Laura knew that it was her father behind the mask of BOB the whole time, Jennifer Lynch remarked, "I could be way off, but part of me is pretty convinced that BOB is as much a creation of Laura's so she doesn't see her father, as BOB is a creation of Leland's, so he's not really doing it. So whatever that evil is, whatever that dysfunction is, it's also that protective mechanism where the two of them have designed it so that there's this dialogue happening. Laura couldn't change who she was, because she was so innocent and young, but she had to change who was hurting her. And Leland as a man and a father and as this broken abuser . . . it had to be given another name and another face. In my consciousness, they both created it, without obviously discussing it."[35] While Lynch's interpretation is certainly interesting, it doesn't take into account that it's not just Leland or Laura who see BOB. Sarah Palmer sees him in the Palmer living room in "Traces to Nowhere" (1.02); Maddy Ferguson encounters him in the Hayward home in "Coma" (2.02); and in "The Condemned Woman" (2.16), Cooper watches as BOB crawls out from beneath Josie Packard's bed, after she dies, screaming, "Coop! What happened to Josie?!" before disappearing. Much like M.C. Blakeman's interpretation of the casket scene, so much of the series is ambiguous and open to interpretation; figuring out where the truth lies and what one wants to believe is part of what makes *Twin Peaks* still so captivating after all these years.

Writer/producer Robert Engels saw things in a somewhat different light. "Both the incest and the violence threw me, because I didn't think of it that way," he recalls. "I was much more in the process of thinking it was BOB inside of Leland. For me, it was more about thinking that Leland was possessed. Clearly I was aware that it was incest. I was more interested in how a being could be inside Leland and how that worked. That helped me write stuff for Leland."[36]

In the contemporary television environment, incest is broached more frequently (where would *Game of Thrones* be without it?) but it was a rarity when *Twin Peaks* took its core mystery into taboo territory, and many were repulsed by the revelation that BOB-as-Leland had been abusing and had murdered his daughter. "One of the things the show did that was very rare in television at that time was the central idea of what was going on with the Laura story: domestic violence and a terrible crime that was going on inside a family," remembers co-creator Mark Frost. "We didn't flinch away from that. And the violence onscreen is the furthest thing from gratuitous but is actually quite horrifying when you actually experience it. And I felt that we were very true to something that meant a lot to a lot of people.

"I didn't have a sense of this at the time, but over the years people that have been through that kind of experience have come forward and told me how powerful of an experience it was to see this in a way that felt truthful to their experience of it, and it was very liberating to see it come out of the darkness, and we talked about it. We were dealing with a tough subject and we wanted to focus on it and clarify it for our films, and sometimes when you reveal something monstrous, you can find a kind of grace for people that helps them cathartically deal with an experience like that."[37]

Frost expanded on those thoughts in a December 2012 interview, saying, "Nothing that dark had ever really been on television for a sustained period of time. But we approached it from a mythic kind of storytelling. We didn't want to tell it like an after-school special would. Here's a social problem and here's a solution. We wanted to approach from the angle of: life is deep and dark and mysterious and sometimes terrible, dreadful unspeakable things happen. I think the show succeeded in doing that. Even though some people thought the show was violent, when there was violence it was for real. It wasn't like fake violence. It was terrifying violence. Because real violence, if you've been near it, is terrifying."[38] And as Sheryl Lee recalled years later, "I have had many people, victims of incest, approach me since the film was released, so glad that it had been made because it helped them to release a lot."[39] The show's ability to explore the darkest recesses of the human soul paved the way for other programs to do the same.

Not all is bleak in *Twin Peaks* when it comes to families, though: family dysfunction is also played for laughs, such as the season two storyline between the Milford brothers, Mayor Dwayne (John Boylan) and Dougie (Tony Jay), the publisher of the *Twin Peaks Gazette*, who has a habit of marrying regularly (every two months, so says his brother). During Dougie's wedding ceremony to the much younger yet alluringly lovely Lana in "Masked Ball" (2.11), Mayor Milford objects to their union, declaring Lana "a gold digger who just wants his money and publishing empire." Sadly, the Mayor may be right — Dougie is found dead in his room at the Great Northern Hotel in the next episode, "The Black Widow" (2.12), surrounded by sex toys, the Kama Sutra, and love poems. As Sheriff Truman declares with a smirk, "It looks like Dougie went out with his boots on." The fact that Mayor Milford winds up in the arms of Lana added some lighter moments as the series headed toward its conclusion.

By redefining the ways that families could be depicted and considered, *Twin Peaks* opened the floodgates for other television shows to do the same. Mark Frost and David Lynch proved that family TV dramas could be as multifaceted as the drama of real families — they could be dark and disturbing, and they could deal with both conventional and taboo topics in unorthodox ways.

6

"The most beautiful dream . . .
and the most terrible nightmare"

So much of *Twin Peaks*' strength and legacy comes from how it twists and plays with conventional forms of storytelling, turning the familiar into something disconcerting and unusual. Equally important is the way in which David Lynch and Mark Frost used the spiritual and supernatural, mixing Eastern mysticism, fairy tales, and occult writings to craft a mythology as perplexing as the mystery that first drew viewers in.

From almost the very beginning of the series, spirituality abounds in *Twin Peaks*. In "Zen, or the Skill to Catch a Killer" (1.03), Cooper and members of the Twin Peaks Sheriff's Department are gathered in a wooded area. A blackboard is set up, with chalk-written names of possible suspects with the letter "J" (in her last diary entry, Laura wrote "nervous about meeting 'J' tonight"). A bottle is placed some distance from the board, and a bucket of rocks stands beside Cooper. Knowing his colleagues (and the *Twin Peaks* audience watching) likely have no idea about the country of Tibet (this episode predated the "free Tibet" movement in American pop culture), Cooper goes about giving a brief history lesson on the plight of the Tibetan people, after which we're suddenly given insight into both the methods Cooper will use to solve the case and his willingness to embrace the weirdness that the show would become renowned for. "Following a dream I had three years ago, I have become deeply moved by the plight of the Tibetan people and have been filled with a desire to help them," Cooper says. "I also awoke from this same dream realizing that I had subconsciously gained knowledge of a certain deductive technique, involving mind-body coordination operating hand-in-hand with the deepest levels of intuition."

Truman reads out the names on the blackboard; Cooper then repeats each name and throws a rock at the bottles. A few miss, one tentatively hits and makes the bottle wobble; eventually Cooper manages direct contact, the bottle shattering in response to the name "Leo Johnson." Truman and company are, like the audience, baffled but intrigued. Cooper's use of Tibetan mysticism is thanks to an encounter David Lynch had with the Dalai Lama. "I went to this place in Hollywood where I met the Dalai Lama," Lynch told Chris Rodley. "And I got fired up about the plight of the Tibetan people. And I told Mark, 'We've got to do something!' And that whole scene developed out of meeting the Dalai Lama! And then it added another layer to Cooper."[40] Mark Frost concurred, later telling Brad Dukes, "David and I shared an interest in Tibet and mysticism so we made that an interest of Cooper's and thought it would be interesting to fold into the traditional, Western-logical detective process we've seen in many characters over the years. Cooper has a layer of intuition that relies on alternate ways of knowing beyond simply being the smart guy and figuring stuff out."[41]

This early use of mysticism cements both Cooper and the series as unorthodox, asking the viewer to take a leap of faith just as Truman and company do. Lynch and Frost know what they're putting onscreen is unusual, just as Cooper knows his methods are strange to his new colleagues. He is as enthusiastic and dogged using this investigative technique as he is with forensic science. In one way, this echoes Frost's beloved Sherlock Holmes and his intuitive and avant-garde style of detective work; in another, it recalls Lynch's style of film-making — trying anything out in a scene or with a character and seeing what sticks. If we're willing to go along for the ride, weird and wonderful things await us.

Cooper acknowledges the power of both his conscious mind and his subconscious, which is on full display at the end of the episode when we enter his dream world. Lying down in his room at the Great Northern, Special Agent Dale Cooper finds himself visited by two mysterious men: Mike, the One-Armed Man (Al Strobel), who recites a poem that ends with "fire walk with me," and BOB, whom we've already seen haunting Sarah Palmer. BOB is a bringer of death; he tells Cooper as much in his dream ("Catch you with my death bag. You may think I've gone insane, but I promise, I will kill again!"). We then enter the Red Room — enclosed by red curtains, a zigzag black-and-white pattern on the floor, a statue of the Venus de Milo, and three chairs that are occupied by Cooper, seemingly aged some 25 years, a woman who appears to be Laura Palmer, and the red-suited character known as the Man from Another Place — his mischievous smile and strange movements taking the moment to a whole new level of strangeness.

The Man from Another Place speaks in a distorted manner; the actor recorded his dialogue backwards, and then the footage was run in reverse. (That task came easily to Anderson who "in junior high had a tape recorder that could run backwards and had learned [to talk backwards] from that."[42]) He tells Cooper that the gum he likes is going to come back into style (at the time, this cryptic "clue" became a much-cited quote that found its way into the pop-culture lexicon, even though audiences would not discover its relevance until "Arbitrary Law," 2.09). When Cooper asks the woman in front of him if she is indeed Laura Palmer, she answers, "I feel like I know her, but sometimes my arms bend back." She looks to be in pain as she motions with her arms. The Man from Another Place then states, "Where we're from, the birds sing a pretty song, and there's always music in the air." With that, he rises from his seat, as jazzy music (courtesy of the show's brilliant composer, Angelo Badalamenti) fills the room, and the Man from Another Place dances, swaying back and forth. Laura (or her doppelgänger) kisses Cooper's mouth softly and whispers something in his ear. Suddenly, Cooper jolts awake (with a fairly wicked cowlick to boot), picks up the phone, and places a call to Sheriff Truman. "Harry, it's Cooper," he begins. "Meet me for breakfast, 7 a.m., the hotel lobby. I know who killed Laura Palmer. [pause] No, it can wait until morning." With that, Cooper begins to snap his fingers in time with the music that plays over the episode's end credits. It's all very cryptic, not to mention creepy, and it's just the beginning. While the audience is aware that we've been inside Cooper's dream space, when he proceeds to incorporate his dreaming into reality, the methodology destabilizes the characters' and audience's grip on reality.

In the following episode, "Rest in Pain" (1.04), Cooper admits that he can't remember the name of the killer. In a wildly surreal show, that moment hit on a familiar truth: what is clear in the space between dreaming and lucidity becomes maddeningly vague in daylight. (It also offers another moment of humor, when both Lucy and Truman utter "damn" at Cooper's failed memory.) Still, the dream space offers up a new set of clues that Cooper investigates: he takes the vision of his dream seriously, leading the audience (and the Sheriff's Department) along on his strange but earnest journey. It's no coincidence that the red curtains of the Black Lodge mirror the curtains at One Eyed Jacks, where both Ronette Pulaski (Phoebe Augustine) and Laura Palmer worked; the Man from Another Place portends the arrival of Maddy Ferguson; and the dance he performs connects to Leland Palmer's constant two-stepping. TV show dream sequences are usually respites from the real world, often used for comedic purposes with little future relevance; on *Twin Peaks*, the unreality of the dream world is significantly important to the series' ongoing narrative. What lurks in the subconscious is equally as important as that which is tangible in the physical realm.

The Man from Another Place, BOB, the Giant who visits Cooper (Carel Struycken) — these characters find precedents in classic strange tales. BOB's constantly leering grin is shades of *Alice's Adventures in Wonderland*'s Cheshire Cat, while the Man from Another Place's stature and cryptic wordplay recall those of the White Rabbit. Cooper's dream world is the proverbial rabbit hole. "When the idea of the Giant came up, we knew he was part of this dream realm that was becoming a big part of *Peaks*," recalled Mark Frost. "We needed entities who could color in and infuse that space with otherworldliness. This is mythological/fairy-tale territory, so a giant was a perfect figure for that purpose."[43]

Lynch has explored fairy-tale otherworlds before: 1990's *Wild at Heart* is the director's take on one of his favorite films, *The Wizard of Oz*. Lula Fortune (Laura Dern) and Sailor Ripley (Nicolas Cage) are on a road trip (their own Yellow Brick Road) in the hopes of escaping Lula's domineering mother, a Wicked Witch of the West type. Sheryl Lee even shows up at the film's climax as Glinda the Good Witch. In both *Wild at Heart* and *Twin Peaks*, these fairy-tale elements act as signposts to the viewer: the journey the characters are taking will be outside the realm of our everyday reality.

Cooper's dream is also our introduction to the Black

Lodge, *Twin Peaks'* version of a haunted house, draped not in black but in red, haunted by the unusual. More than simply a place contrived in Cooper's dreams, we learn as the series progresses that it's the mythological meeting place for the evil that surrounds Twin Peaks. In "The One-Armed Man" (1.05), Sheriff Truman reveals to Agent Cooper that the citizens of Twin Peaks have long been aware that "there's a sort of evil out there. Something very strange in these old woods. Call it what you want — a darkness, a presence. It takes many forms but it's been out there for as long as anybody can remember. But we've always been here to fight it." The "we" Truman refers to is the Bookhouse Boys. In the process of investigating Laura Palmer's murder, Cooper, Truman, and the Boys begin to unravel the secrets of the Black Lodge and its mirror, the White Lodge. In "Variations on Relations" (2.19), Windom Earle describes the White Lodge as a proverbial Garden of Eden, where "the sounds of innocence and joy filled the air. And when it rained, it rained sweet nectar that infused one's heart with a desire to live life in truth and beauty. Generally speaking, a ghastly place, reeking of virtue's sour smell." For Earle, it's the Black Lodge that holds the real allure, "a place of almost unimaginable power, chock-full of dark forces and vicious secrets. No prayers dare enter this frightful maw. The spirits there care not for good deeds or priestly invocations; they're as like to rip the flesh from your bone as greet you with a happy 'good day.'"

While Earle speaks both reverentially and menacingly of the Black Lodge, in "Masked Ball" (2.11), Deputy Hawk and his Native American brethren also know of the supernatural place, with their own interpretation of what the lodge is. "[The Black Lodge is] the shadow-self of the White Lodge," he tells Cooper. "The legend says that every spirit must pass through there on the way to perfection. There, you will meet your own shadow self. My people call it 'the Dweller on the Threshold.'" While some of *Twin Peaks*' mythology was created for the show, a good portion of it is a pastiche of ideas unfamiliar to a mainstream audience. Take, for instance, "the Dweller on the Threshold" to which Hawk refers — that comes from 19th century theosophical literature, referring to an invisible malevolent entity that attaches itself to a human being. On *Twin Peaks*, the dweller is BOB, who had attached himself to Leland, yearned to be inside Laura, and killed her when he couldn't have her. Ultimately, the dweller takes over Cooper. Windom Earle also makes reference to black wizards or "dugpas" who can be found within the Black Lodge. In her 1918 book, *The Theosophical Glossary*, infamous Russian occultist Madame Helena Blavatsky (a favorite of conspiracy theorists to this day) gives the term "dugpa" multiple meanings, with it representing both the Tibetan word for thunder and a Buddhist sorcerer. Meanwhile, legendary Beat writer William S. Burroughs makes references to both a Black and a White Lodge in his 1981 novel, *Cities of the Red Night*. As the author of *The List of Seven* (1993), a novel that draws directly on occultism and theosophy, all of these influences were directly in Mark Frost's wheelhouse. When asked if it is fair to assume he was familiar with the work of "dark" writers such as

Madame Blavatsky, along with the man known as "The Beast," Aleister Crowley, Frost agreed, stating that it was "more than fair."[44] Meanwhile, as someone deeply entrenched in the study and practice of Transcendental Meditation, David Lynch would likely have also come across the writings of Blavatsky and Crowley in the course of his life.

The Judeo-Christian Bible also finds its way into *Twin Peaks'* potpourri of spirituality. Sarah Palmer twice sees a white horse: just prior to Maddy's murder and, in *Twin Peaks: Fire Walk with Me*, in the moments before Laura's death. For symbolists, the horse might represent the one Death rides in on in Book of Revelations: "And I looked, and behold a pale horse: and his name that sat on him was Death, and Hell followed with him. And power was given unto them over the fourth part of the earth, to kill with sword, and with hunger, and with death, and with the beasts of the earth."[45] In *The Secret Diary of Laura Palmer*, Laura writes of a horse (cinnamon, not white) given to her by her father (though she soon discovers the gift actually came from Benjamin Horne). Laura spends time with her horse as refuge from the increasing darkness that is growing within her. The animal seems to represent innocence to both Laura and her mother. The same holds true for Maddy, who upon telling her Aunt Sarah and Uncle Leland that she'd be returning home to Missoula, comfortingly adds, "I'll come galloping back often!" ("Lonely Souls," 2.07).

Trying to decode the iconography of *Twin Peaks* has been a hobby of the show's enthusiasts for 25 years now. The series never explains the symbolism of the white horse or the owls (the animal manifestation of evil, perhaps?) or anything else explicitly, but the possibilities are myriad. The beauty of this approach is that, should one wish to dig deeper into possible meanings, there is much to discover and interpret. On the flip side, nothing is ever lost by simply embracing what's seen onscreen. The show that fused mysticism, spirituality, the supernatural, and the occult ventured beyond the conventional, into the subconscious, to explore that which cannot be rationally explained.

7

"A large and interesting place"

In April 2013, Hannibal Lecter returned to the small screen in the hands of noted television creator Bryan Fuller, the man responsible for cult-favorite programs *Wonderfalls*, *Pushing Daisies*, and *Dead Like Me*. *Hannibal* pushed both storytelling conventions and violence to places that NBC had rarely, if ever, gone before; this is a show about serial killers, and their work is always graphically on display. The show's visual language, from its dream space to its visual cues, is more than a little familiar in its peculiarity. With so much creativity and experimentation, I couldn't help wondering what had inspired Fuller. The answer wasn't all that surprising.

In an interview with Melanie Votaw, Fuller explained, "When I sat down to the script, I was very consciously saying, 'What would David Lynch do with a Hannibal Lecter character? What sort of strange, unexpected places would he take this world?' I'm a great admirer of his work and his aesthetic and his meticulous sound design. Those were all components that I felt very strongly needed to be part of our Hannibal Lecter story. Between Lynch and [Stanley] Kubrick, there's a lot of inspiration."[46]

What would David Lynch do? It's not only a question that would make an excellent bumper sticker, but one that, prior to *Twin Peaks* airing between 1990 and 1991, nobody working on network television would ever have considered asking. But in the 25 years since *Twin Peaks* debuted, creators who were exposed to the world of Agent Cooper and Laura Palmer have found inspiration in Lynch and Frost's willingness to push the boundaries. At the same time, the images and iconography of *Twin Peaks* — the Black Lodge and the Man from Another Place — have become prime pop culture touchstones, ripe for loving parody or blatant pilfering.

It must be noted, though, that at the time of its demise, few would have expected *Twin Peaks* to continue to resonate with audiences. After the phenomenal response to the first season, the backlash against season two was severe. Writer/producer Harley Peyton, alongside Robert Engels and Mark Frost, kept *Twin Peaks* moving during that period, even as audience interest waned. Unsurprisingly, Peyton is more inclined to recollect the (many) good aspects from the last half of the series than to dwell upon its perceived failure. "The first seven episodes of the second season leading up to the death of Leland Palmer, I would put up against any television show in the history of television," says Peyton. "I think the second season is underrated. It became sort of fashionable to say, 'The first season was awesome; the second one was terrible.' There was still pretty good stuff going on, lots of fun stuff that people forget about, including David Duchovny as the transvestite FBI agent. When had that been done before? And then you get to the last episode. We each wrote an act, but then David [Lynch] came in, tossed everything out the window, and said, 'Yeah, I'm not doing this.' That's the only time that happened. At the time it was like, 'Aw, fuck him, what's he doing?' And then you saw the result and went 'OK.' It took it to another level. Even though none of us wanted the show to end, it was the perfect ending for it."[47]

Broadcast on June 10, 1991, *Twin Peaks'* final episode was viewed by 10.4 million people, an impressive number by today's standards but down considerably from the 34.6 million who had viewed the pilot one year earlier. As the final moments ran out, the audience was left with Agent Cooper possessed by BOB, blood running from his forehead, first laughing at his reflection and then turning his head ever so slightly to face the audience, with the question, "How's Annie?" The episode, directed by David Lynch, was undeniably as strong and hypnotic as anything the series had achieved before; it just came far too late for it to matter to anyone except the diehards.

There was some hope for fans when David Lynch announced he would be revisiting the town with *Twin Peaks: Fire Walk with Me*, a feature-length film that would cover the final seven days in the life of Laura Palmer. It's a harrowing film, one that sadly didn't find an audience when it was released at the tail end of summer 1992, a year after *Twin Peaks'* finale. While fans and critics were expecting the film to pick up on the many cliffhangers that the series left us with, and to bring back all of the show's beloved characters, David Lynch was more interested in illuminating the pieces of Laura Palmer's life that had previously only been hinted at. "At the end of the series I felt sad," said Lynch. "I couldn't get myself to leave the world of *Twin Peaks*. I was in love with the character of Laura Palmer and her contradictions, radiant on the surface but dying inside. I wanted to see her live, move, and talk."[48]

Though many series regulars shot scenes for the film, gone in the final cut were core characters like Benjamin Horne, Sheriff Truman, Audrey Horne, and Pete Martell. Also missing was the series' quirky and endearing sense of humor and strangeness that fans had fallen in love with. Instead, Lynch went full throttle in uncovering the darkness of the town and within Laura's mind. We're given an uncensored look into life in the Palmer household, which is absolutely brimming with terror as disturbing as anything from a horror film. Prior to the movie, which was written by Lynch and *Twin Peaks* writer/producer Robert Engels, fans never had the opportunity to see the way Leland, Laura, and Sarah interacted with one another, but in *Twin Peaks: Fire Walk with Me*, we witness a variety of truly frightening family moments. In the most memorable, at the Palmer dining room table, Leland berates Laura for not washing her hands before sitting down for dinner and demands to know who gave her the heart locket hanging around her neck, just as Sarah walks into the room.

LELAND

Oh, is this from a lover? Did you get this from your lover?

SARAH

They don't call them lovers in high school, Leland.

LELAND

Bobby didn't give this to you.

SARAH

How do you know that Bobby didn't give it to her?

The questioning reveals how desperate BOB is to know everything about Laura, and how powerless Laura is against him. The horror in the room reaches fever pitch, as Leland pinches the frightened Laura's cheek and Sarah begs Leland to stop.

LELAND

Did Bobby give you this or is there someone new?

SARAH

Leland leave her alone . . . she doesn't like that.

LELAND

How do you know what she likes?

SARAH

Stop it!

It's a horrible, riveting, powerful moment of a family on the brink of something terrible, and each actor plays their role amazingly well. Grace Zabriskie's Sarah Palmer is so very out of control throughout all of *Twin Peaks*, but this scene in particular finds her trying to hold herself and her family together with some semblance of normalcy, something that the series never allowed for. Meanwhile, with the way his eyes change and body shifts, Ray Wise moves from an everyman to a malevolent evil with remarkable ease. As Wise would recall in 2013, "There were certain moments during the film where I would have to flip the switch from being good Leland, saying, 'Oh hello, honey, princess, darling' to [BOB] . . . it was a totally different acting problem, a totally different character [from the show], because I was in the dark for most of the series."[49]

Finally, Sheryl Lee is tasked with playing a character who is strong and independent at one moment, and then trapped and frightened the next. In *Twin Peaks: Fire Walk with Me*, watching Wise and Lee together as father and daughter is a revelation — two souls doing battle with their inner demons. For all the criticisms the film would receive for what it wasn't, it's certainly deserving of praise for how Lynch and Engels were able to craft a father-daughter relationship like no other on film.

However, once *Twin Peaks: Fire Walk with Me* hit theaters, it appeared as if no one was satisfied with the final product. Critics savaged the film (unjustly in many people's minds) for lacking the humor of the original series, and it was virtually ignored (everywhere except for Japan, where it was actually a hit). Legend has it that the film was so reviled that it was booed at its premiere at the Cannes Film Festival. Not true, says co-writer Robert Engels. "I was there," said Engels in October 2013. "They didn't. Nobody booed. I feel bad for David, because it didn't happen that way."[50] However, the film's legacy has grown over time, with many (myself included) citing it as their favorite Lynch film.

While the boos at Cannes may have been a myth, the truth was, when it came to David Lynch and his North American audience, the bloom was off the rose. The toast of mainstream Hollywood just a few years earlier, Lynch was now a victim of the media machine, at least in the mind of colleague Engels. "America does this to people," he said. "People get declared geniuses and then there's a certain part of the population that has to beat them down because they can't be [geniuses] the whole time."[51] Following that scathing reaction to *Twin Peaks: Fire Walk with Me*, it would be five years until Lynch would release another feature film.

While the cast and crew were moving on from *Twin Peaks*, the show itself continued to linger on, its inspiration and language often showing up in the most unexpected of places. In 1992, an episode of Disney's animated series *Darkwing Duck* was titled "Twin Beaks," and was full of nods to our favorite TV show, everything from references to "great pie and darn good coffee" to the character of Launchpad conversing with a silent log, which tells him, "The cows are not what they seem." While not the first children's show to parody *Twin Peaks* (that honor goes to *Sesame Street*'s own "Twin Beaks" in 1991), it certainly is one of the strangest (and on a Disney show, no less). The kids watching may not have been aware of the homage, but parents watching beside them would have gotten a chuckle out of it.

In *Twin Peaks*' wake, "quirky" television shows began springing up, many of them hailed by critics as "the next *Twin Peaks*." Knowing that there was an audience that was at least open-minded to a television series that strayed from the norm, two years after *Twin Peaks* premiered, CBS debuted *Picket Fences*, created by David E. Kelley, who had previously written for *L.A. Law*, co-created *Doogie Howser, M.D.*, and would go on to spearhead later TV blockbusters like *Ally McBeal*, *The Practice*, and *Boston Legal*. For his first solo kick at the prime-time can, Kelley's *Picket Fences* featured grizzled Hollywood actor Tom Skerritt as the sheriff of another small town, Rome, Wisconsin — home to the "serial bathers," the Green Bay Chopper (a serial who chops off the right hands of their victims), and many other offbeat characters. After an early struggle in the ratings, *Picket Fences* found its own sure footing and lasted four well-regarded seasons.

Another CBS series that was saddled with *Twin Peaks* comparisons was *Northern Exposure*, a 1990 summer replacement series that debuted just three months after the *Twin Peaks* pilot aired, about a New York City doctor forced to move to Cicely, Alaska, to practice medicine to pay off his student loan. The cleverly comedic *Northern Exposure* lasted six seasons, the focus eventually shifting from Rob Morrow's young Dr. Fleischman to the eclectic group of people who lived in the town. *Northern Exposure* proudly wore the *Twin Peaks* comparisons on its proverbial sleeve, paying homage to it during "The Russian Flu," the fifth episode of the show's first season, which aired complete with *Twin Peaks*–style music and visuals, references to coffee, donuts, and cherry pie, and even a mention of a woman carrying a log.

Picket Fences and *Northern Exposure* lasted significantly longer than *Twin Peaks*, in large part because both series, while somewhat similar in tone to the show's first season, never veered into the darkest territory that *Twin Peaks* covered. The visual language wasn't there, but the quirkiness was, making both much more palatable to the masses.

The most successful of the *Twin Peaks*–influenced television series of the early '90s was *The X-Files*, created by a former Disney TV screenwriter named Chris Carter. With two FBI agents, skeptic Dana Scully and card-carrying extraterrestrial believer Fox Mulder (*Twin Peaks* alum David Duchovny), acting as our point of entry, *The X-Files* evolved from a monster-of-the-week formula to a show with its own full-blown mythology revolving around aliens, abductions, government cover-ups, and much, much more. Like *Twin Peaks*, nothing on *The X-Files* was ever as it seemed. Though oftentimes convoluted, with its own unanswered questions and characters, *The X-Files* became a massive success over the course of nine seasons, 202 episodes, and two feature films. Many were quick to point out the connection between *The X-Files* and *Twin Peaks*. In 2002, Joyce Millman of the *New York Times* wrote that *The X-Files* "owed an obvious debt to the freaky metaphysical mysteries of *Twin Peaks* — that show's quirky Agent Cooper and Fox Mulder could have been spiritual twins."[52] Throughout its run, the series was unafraid to take chances with its stories, though, unlike *Twin Peaks*, *The X-Files* and its creators never seemed to bow to the pressure to solve its mysteries.

During the summer of 1995, following the sixth-season finale of *The Simpsons*, the biggest mystery on television was "Who shot Mr. Burns?" (spoofing the "Who shot J.R.?" phenomenon some 15 years earlier). Speculation ran high as to which one of Springfield's citizens had pulled the trigger on Montgomery Burns, and when the series returned a few months later, it came complete with a brilliant parody of the classic Red Room scene from *Twin Peaks*, during which Chief Wiggum meets a dancing, backwards-talking Lisa Simpson, who offers him some not-so-cryptic help in solving the mystery. In true *Simpsons* fashion, the writers went to great lengths to ensure authenticity with its parody, including a shadow floating past the curtains of the room, right down to Yeardley Smith recording her dialogue as Lisa backwards and then having it reversed, the same technique used for Michael J. Anderson's the Man from Another Place. Amazingly, they even thought to give Wiggum a cowlick when he wakes up from his dream. As if to reaffirm that the *Twin Peaks* love was no fluke, seven years after the show's premiere, *The Simpsons* would once again pay homage to the series in yet another episode, "Lisa's Sax"; in this instance, Homer Simpson is seen watching *Twin Peaks*: the Giant who visited Agent Cooper in the second-season premiere is onscreen dancing with a white horse. A hypnotized Homer simply remarks, "Brilliant . . . I have absolutely no idea what's going on."

It wasn't just on television that *Twin Peaks* was still resonating. In 2007, the Twin Peaks Definitive Gold Box Edition was released, compiling the entire series on DVD, complete with both the broadcast and European versions of the pilot, mini-documentaries, and deleted scenes. David Lynch, often reluctant to revisit his past work and very protective of the series (at one point refusing to allow a potential third-season comic book), was hands-on with the Gold Box, filming new extras while supervising all of its visual upgrades. Not only did the collection sell well, demonstrating that there was still a huge appetite for the series, it also became a prime example of how to repackage a TV series on DVD.

Meanwhile, that same year, a trailer appeared on YouTube for a video game called *Rainy Woods*, which had unabashedly pulled its main imagery from the television show. Within its one-minute-and-30-second run time, images of a red room, complete with two twins who looked exactly like the Man from Another Place, are on display. An autopsy is being conducted on a woman who bears a striking resemblance to Laura Palmer. We have an FBI agent and a sheriff working together, a bumbling deputy, ambient music, and even a chanteuse much like the one who appears at the Roadhouse. It was enough to get *Twin Peaks* fans salivating at the thought of entering a world that resembled the one they loved. However, as word spread about *Rainy Woods* and its similarity to the show, the developers made the legally responsible move to make serious amendments to the game. The red curtains were removed, and the older male twins in suits became younger twin boys, while the game's name changed to *Deadly Premonition*. However, when it was finally released for the Xbox 360 in 2010, the influence of *Twin Peaks* was still front and center, especially with the character of FBI Special Agent Francis York Morgan, who receives special messages from the cups of coffee he constantly craves.

Undeniably weird, *Deadly Premonition* quickly became one of the most divisive video games in history. While some reviewers gave it perfect marks for its open-world storytelling and obvious *Twin Peaks*–inspired quirkiness, others criticized its low-definition graphics and clunky game play. As a result, *Deadly Premonition* actually made it into the *Guinness World Records Gamer's Edition*, where it was honored with the title of "Most Critically Polarizing Survival Horror Game." Like the series that spawned it, *Deadly Premonition* has gone on to become a cult classic, receiving a director's cut treatment in 2013 on the Playstation 3, and even sparking talk of a sequel. For *Twin Peaks* fans craving an official video game, it will have to do.

The same year that *Deadly Premonition* was inciting debate among gamers and critics around the world, another television show was paying tribute to the series, generating a ton of publicity for itself and *Twin Peaks* in the process. Broadcast on December 1, 2010, on the USA Network, "Dual Spires" was the 12th episode of the fifth season of *Psych*, a reasonably popular comedy about two best friends who solve crimes as consultants for the Santa Barbara Police Force — Shawn

Spencer (James Roday), who uses his keen observational skills to convince people he has psychic abilities, and Shawn's best friend and partner, Burton "Gus" Guster (Dulé Hill). In this episode, Shawn and Gus are drawn to the small town of Dual Spires to attend a cinnamon festival, where they're soon called upon to investigate the murder of a teenage girl, Paula Merral (an anagram for Laura Palmer).

Growing up, James Roday was an admitted *Twin Peaks* fan and had been keen on paying homage to the show since the first season of *Psych*. During promotion for the episode, Roday, who co-wrote the episode, told reporters, "*Twin Peaks* is my favorite show of all time, hands down . . . It just took three more years for us to gain enough steam and get enough fans and have enough sea legs to actually be able to pull something like that off. It was worth the wait because I think it came out way better than it would have if we tried to do it too soon."[53] The tribute episode of *Psych* managed to snag various *Twin Peaks* alumni for roles, including Sheryl Lee, Ray Wise (who had previously appeared on *Psych* and returned as the same character), Sherilyn Fenn, and Dana Ashbrook. Catherine Coulson's Log Lady has a cameo, walking through the town of Dual Spires carrying a piece of wood, while the familiar voice of Julee Cruise sings the show's opening theme in a style paying homage to her work with *Twin Peaks* composer Angelo Badalamenti. Along with the recognizable sounds and faces, the episode has numerous allusions to Roday's favorite show, from the town newspaper being called the *Great Northern* to the discovery of the body wrapped in plastic (not to mention

Dana Ashbrook's character's overwhelming crying fit when said body is found). The series went to town with its final scene, in which, according to an "enhanced" Dual Spires video found at the *Psych* website, there are more than 724 references to *Twin Peaks*, from giants to One Eyed Jacks.

The Dual Spires episode of *Psych* did well in the ratings and received positive reviews from critics who were impressed with the loving care put into paying tribute to one of television's most influential shows. Clearly, the creators were devoted fans, as they managed to nail many of the endearing and enduring eccentricities that *Twin Peaks* fans had fallen in love with. For some of the alums that guest-starred, it was also a fond, yet surreal experience. As the character of Donna "Doc" Gooden, Sheryl Lee was the one to discover the body of Paula Merral; while filming that particular scene, Lee couldn't help flashing back to her own experience wrapped in plastic, nearly 20 years earlier. "I actually did feel as if I was out of my body, that whole day [of shooting]," she told *Collider* in 2010. "It was a very strange, surreal feeling, mostly because it's hard to understand how that much time went by that quickly. I remember that day, as if it was yesterday. There are a lot of things in the past 20 years that I don't remember, but that day, 20 years ago, lying on that beach in the freezing cold, I remember as if it was yesterday. So, it was very surreal, and it touched me deeper than I expected it to. It snuck up on me."[54]

Twin Peaks' influence, imagery, and iconography has never really gone away; sometimes it's there, even when a creator says it isn't. In the fourth-season finale of *Buffy the*

Vampire Slayer, "Restless," each member of the Scooby gang (Buffy Summers; her best friends, Willow and Xander; and her mentor, Giles) encounters the same malevolent entity in their dreams. The various dream sequences reference classic Hammer films, *Apocalypse Now*, and *Twin Peaks*. There's a man in a suit waving slices of cheese around, and Willow ventures through red curtains during her dream. Though creator Joss Whedon downplayed any direct correlation between these images and *Twin Peaks*, the fact is, when any television series uses surreal or head-scratching dream sequences or imagery, Mark Frost and David Lynch's work is always at least a partial inspiration.

David Chase, the creator of *The Sopranos*, has referred to his landmark show as *"Twin Peaks* in New Jersey," allegedly citing the show's dream sequence as the greatest in television history. Chase offered up his own classic dream sequence during "The Test Dream," a season-five episode of *The Sopranos* that received not only rave reviews, but also the requisite *Twin Peaks* comparisons. In his biography of David Lynch, Greg Olson shrewdly notes that Chase's 2004 description of the artistry of television sounds like something David Lynch might say: "Television shows are usually full of talk. I think there should be strong visuals on a show, some sense of mystery to it, connections that don't add up. I think there should be dreams and music and dead air and stuff that goes nowhere. There should be, God forbid, a little bit of poetry."[55]

For other creators, watching *Twin Peaks* had a fundamental impact on their future ambitions. Case in point: Damon

Lindelof, the co-creator of the often brilliant and occasionally divisive ABC series *Lost*. In 2010, during an edition of TimesTalk Live, Lindelof was asked which show he watched growing up that made him want to create his own series. "*Twin Peaks* was a huge impact on me," he replied. "I would watch it with my dad, and when the show was over, we would talk for two hours about what the hell just happened . . . the sort of fundamental idea that a television show could leave the space of the hour it was on and enter into a conversation with other people as to what it meant . . . the question of who killed Laura Palmer became so secondary to all these other sorts of mysteries that were swirling around it, I just remember wanting to meet David Lynch and ask him questions about his show. That was sort of my first fundamental understanding that TV was actually made up by people."[56]

Lindelof's *Lost* colleague, showrunner and writer Carlton Cuse, was equally effusive with his praise for *Twin Peaks* when discussing *Bates Motel*, the prequel series to *Psycho*, adapted from Robert Bloch's novel, that Cuse executive-produced for A&E alongside former *Friday Night Lights* writer Kerry Ehrin. "I would say that the content of the show is probably one part *Friday Night Lights*, one part *Lost*, and one part *Twin Peaks*," Cuse told *Entertainment Weekly*. "I think that *Twin Peaks* was definitely an influence for both of us. It was a show that was super intriguing and seemed to have tremendous possibilities . . . we also liked the idea that there's two parts to every person. There's the superficial veneer, which in this town is the very beautiful bucolic place and everybody seems great, but underneath that all these characters have these dark desires and secrets. We felt like that would be a wonderful territory in which to land Norma and Norman." Ehrin concurred, stating, "The really cool thing about *Twin Peaks* is the town of it allowed people to act in a strange way without judging them. That's important in this too."[57] Cuse took his praise even further during a May 2013 *Bates Motel* panel discussion at the Paley Center in Los Angeles, where he jokingly told the gathered audience, "We pretty much ripped off *Twin Peaks*. If you wanted to get that confession, the answer is yes. I loved that show. They only did 30 episodes. Kerry and I thought we'd do the 70 that are missing."[58]

While shows like *The X-Files*, *Lost*, and *Bates Motel* found inspiration and built upon the foundation *Twin Peaks* had laid out, one of its closest cousins, at least thematically, didn't quite learn from the perceived mistakes it had made. In 2011, *The Killing* began airing on AMC. An adaptation of a Dutch television show, *The Killing* initially revolves around the murder of a teenage girl, Rosie Larsen, and the police investigation that follows. Much like *Twin Peaks*, the series deals with the repercussions of Larsen's killing and the effect it has on her family. Amazingly, executive producer Veena Sud pleaded ignorance to any connections between *The Killing* and *Twin Peaks*, telling *Entertainment Weekly* in 2011, "I have never seen *Twin Peaks*. I heard that [there were similarities]. I assumed because we're set in Seattle and there's a young girl that's been murdered, I think maybe it's natural people would compare shows because you don't often see dark, brooding cop shows set in Seattle."[59]

The show's sell line of "Who killed Rosie Larsen?" bore a remarkable resemblance to "Who killed Laura Palmer?" and it appeared that those marketing *The Killing* hadn't learned from *Twin Peaks'* experience. Their whodunit-focused campaign also backfired by creating expectations for answers that went unrealized. Though initially well regarded, as the series progressed, critics and audiences became frustrated with *The Killing's* use of increasingly implausible red herrings, along with the perceived lack of resolution to the murder. By the time *The Killing's* dwindling audience finally discovered who killed Rosie Larsen at the end of its second season, few seemed to care. The show received a last-minute reprieve from cancelation and embarked upon a new storyline for its third season, but the damage had been done; *The Killing* was put out of its misery in the summer of 2013, though Netflix picked the show up for a fourth and final season.

In the new millennium, one doesn't have to look too hard on television to see the hallmarks of *Twin Peaks* — even on the likes of ABC Family, where *Pretty Little Liars* trots out the odd homage to the iconic series, as it did with its own murder mystery clue–providing myna bird. As both David Lynch's daughter and Laura Palmer's de facto chronicler, Jennifer Lynch has never had any doubt of the influence the show has had since first airing. "I see it in every good show I see. I see it in *The Sopranos* and *Six Feet Under*. I see it in *Luther*. I see it in *Sherlock*. I see it in *The Killing*. I see it in *Breaking Bad*. Because what it did was, it said, you can do this here. [TV] doesn't have to be the *Sonny and Cher* show all the time. And it doesn't have to be *Good Times*. There was nothing wrong with those shows, but there was a real forum here for reaching in and getting people where they sat in their underwear, at home, and you could whisper to them and talk about things that only certain independent films talked about. And suddenly you were talking about them in your own house, and they had a bigger impact. *Twin Peaks* allowed human beings to start showing up on TV."[60]

For Michael J. Anderson, the show continues to resonate strongly because of how it was "something so non-derivative that it cut its own genre."[61] For writer/producer Robert Engels, the show has survived in pop culture because, as David Lynch himself had said about the show, it was, "cool people doing cool things." Anderson continued: "Even BOB is cool. I think the angst of those people is real. It's like seeing a play that's 40 years old and you're stunned that you're so moved by it. And that's credit to David and Mark that it so captured something about human nature that lasts. I have students, and once a year someone will say, 'My parents watched your show.' And then they say, 'I watched the pilot last night and it was pretty good,' and then two weeks later they'll say, 'I'm on the 13th episode. God, it's really good.' It just speaks to a human emotion that's timeless. It seems so real. There is a Bobby in every high school class: he's a cool guy, and you like him because he's messed up. He's not just what he says he is. I think with the case of *Twin Peaks*, we had such an opportunity to do that for a whole series, and thanks to Mark and David, it held up."[62]

Looking back 25 years later, James Marshall commented

that the series is "its own sort of brilliance. It shifted so many different parts of television. It just changed everything."[63] Kimmy Robertson expressed a similar sentiment, stating, "It's a complete package that was interesting and that hadn't been done before, and David Lynch put his artistic stamp on it. Mark Frost knew how to make things interesting for television. It was time and we were there, and it all just worked out."[64]

After so many years, *Twin Peaks* still manages to influence the artists and audiences who first fell under its spell. When rumors of a supposed Lynch meeting with NBC about a third season broke on December 31, 2012, the internet was immediately aflutter, leading Mark Frost to quickly refute the reports. Considering the influence and the way the show has grown in stature, it's no surprise that diehard fans were constantly hoping for some return to *Twin Peaks*, though at the time Jennifer Lynch said nobody should hold their breath, believing that audiences are better served living in the here and now. "Let's say Grandma was wonderful, and we loved Grandma. And then Grandma died. We can talk about Grandma, but we don't want to dig Grandma up. Grandma would be different now if she came back. It would be a different show; they would make it with new actors. I don't think there's anything more to say. I've heard it from the horse's mouth, there's nothing in the works. What on earth do people think would happen now? Everybody's different. You can't go back there."[65]

Or can you?

Of all of Lynch's projects, *Twin Peaks* has been the one that he always seems to revisit in some form or another. When the Bravo network began replaying the series in its entirety in June 1993 as part of its TV Too Good for TV campaign, each episode came with the added bonus of an introduction from Catherine Coulson's Log Lady. Adding to their authenticity was the fact that David Lynch actually directed each of these brief instalments. While he had been much less involved in the show's second season, it was clear that *Twin Peaks* was still in the back of Lynch's mind, even after all of the drama surrounding its demise. In 2007, when the Definitive Gold Box Edition was released, Lynch took part in a strange *Twin Peaks* reunion filmed for the collection. Set in a dimly lit, smoke-filled bar, Lynch reminisced about the series with Kyle MacLachlan and Mädchen Amick, with the director remarking toward the end of the segment just how much he still loves the world of *Twin Peaks*. Flash-forward to 2014, when Lynch was drawn back to the town yet again, this time facilitating the release of a Blu-Ray collection of the series, complete with new footage of Lynch sitting down to interview Ray Wise, Sheryl Lee, and Grace Zabriskie, both as themselves and as the characters they played on the series and in the film. In typical Lynch fashion, the actors weren't told until the day of shooting that they'd be reprising their iconic roles, when they were given a script that Lynch had come up with. The set also included the Holy Grail for fans — 90 minutes of alternate and deleted scenes from *Fire Walk with Me* that feature many characters not in the final film, including Pete Martell, Josie Packard, and the entire Sheriff's Department. For all intents and purposes, the Blu-Ray release and its new features seemed to mark the end of the *Twin Peaks* story. But even with all the denials of any sort of series continuation or revival, in May 2013, at the Orange County Museum of Modern Art's annual Art of Dining gala, Lynch himself made an offhand remark to Ray Wise about a potential return to the series. Wise reported on *The Ron Purtee Show* that Lynch had said to him, "Well, Ray, you know, the town is still there. And I suppose it's possible that we could revisit it. Of course, you're already dead . . . but we could maybe work around that."[66]

All the speculation and hope was rewarded when on October 6, 2014, David Lynch and Mark Frost announced that they will craft nine new episodes of the series, to air on Showtime in 2016. Familiar faces will return. Questions will be answered and, no doubt, even more will be asked.

If there's one thing we know for sure about *Twin Peaks*, it's that nothing is ever as we expect. With the spectacularly creative team of David Lynch and Mark Frost lighting the way, the original 30 episodes became landmarks in the art of television, breaking ground with their approach to character, storytelling, and visual style. Conventions of network television were twisted, and boundaries broken, and *Twin Peaks* proved that TV could be much more than it had been. After more than two decades, *Twin Peaks* continues to entrance the uninitiated viewer, who can't help but fall under the spell of the small town where the owls are never what they seem.

*Notes

1 Derek P. Rucas, "The Role of Television as a Symbol for 1950s Ideology," *Film Articles and Critiques* (2003).

2 David Lynch and Chris Rodley, *Lynch on Lynch, Revised Edition* (New York: Faber and Faber, 2005), 10.

3 "Exclusive Interview with *Twin Peaks* Co-Creator Mark Frost!" *Brad D Studios*, January 9, 2012, http://braddstudios.com/2012/01/09/exclusive -interview-with-twin-peaks-co-creator-mark-frost.

4 Sean Morrow, "He Killed Laura Palmer: A Talk with *Twin Peaks* Co-Creator Mark Frost," *Portable.tv*, December 5, 2012, http://portable.tv/culture/post/ he-killed-laura-palmer-a-talk-with-twin-peaks-co-creator-mark-frost.

5 Del Howison, "Mark Frost Talks Creating 'Twin Peaks,' Pushing the Boundaries of Television," *Fearnet* (site discontinued).

6 Troy Patterson and Jeff Jensen, "Our Town," *Entertainment Weekly*, Spring 2000.

7 Patterson and Jensen.

8 Jim Jerome, "The Triumph of *Twin Peaks*," *Entertainment Weekly*, April 6, 1990.

9 Christina Radish, "James Roday and Sheryl Lee Interview, *Psych*: A *Twin Peaks* Reunion" *Collider*, http://collider.com/james-roday-sheryl-lee-interview -psych.

10 Patterson and Jensen.

11 Lynch and Rodley, 165.

12 "The Halloween Interview with Michael J. Anderson!" *Brad D Studios*, October 30, 2011, http://braddstudios.com/2011/10/30/the-halloween -interview-with-michael-j-anderson.

13 Keith Phipps, "*Twin Peaks*: Episode 1/Episode 2," *The A.V. Club*, December 5, 2007.

14 Jen Chaney, "*Twin Peaks*: Celebrating the dream sequence on its 21st anniversary," *The Washington Post*, April 19, 2011, http://www.washingtonpost .com/blogs/celebritology/post/twin-peaks-celebrating-the-dream-sequence- on-its-21st-anniversary/2011/04/19/AF2QbS5D_blog.html.

15 "David Lynch: *Twin Peaks* Bob (1997)," YouTube video, posted by Blackdog TV, September 13, 2012, https://www.youtube.com/watch?v=35JZG3CdiWE.

16 Lynch and Rodley, 170.

17 Author interview.

18 Author interview.

19 Author interview.

20 Brad Dukes, "Exclusive Sheryl Lee Interview!! (Part One)," *Twin Peaks Archive*, http://twinpeaksarchive.blogspot.ca/2013/05/exclusive-sheryl-lee-interview-part-one.html.

21 Lynch and Rodley, 175.

22 Michael Giltz, "'Twin Peaks' revisited: 'Maybe we shouldn't have solved the mystery,'" *Los Angeles Times*, August 23, 2010, http://herocomplex.latimes.com/tv/return-to-twin-peaks-a-tv-landmark-20-years-later.

23 "Exclusive Interview with *Twin Peaks* Co-Creator Mark Frost."

24 Author interview.

25 "Lesli Linka Glatter on *Twin Peaks*," *Fast Cheap Movie Thoughts*, June 6, 2013, http://fastcheapmoviethoughts.blogspot.ca/2013/06/lesli-linka-glatter-on-twin-peaks.html.

26 Howison.

27 Author interview.

28 Author interview.

29 Author interview.

30 Author interview.

31 Lynch and Rodley, 182.

32 M.C. Blakeman, "The Awful Truth in *Twin Peaks*," *Chicago Tribune*, November 28, 1990.

33 Author interview.

34 Author interview.

35 Author interview.

36 Author interview.

37 Morrow.

38 Howison.

39 David Hughes, *The Complete Lynch* (London: Virgin, 2001), 179.

40 Lynch and Rodley, 168.

41 Brad Dukes, *Reflections: An Oral History of Twin Peaks* (Chicago: Short/Tall Press, 2014), 80.

42 Author interview.

43 Dukes, *Reflections*, 169.

44 Author Twitter interaction with Mark Frost, October 11, 2013.

45 King James Bible, Revelations 6:8.

46 Melanie Votaw, "Exclusive Interview: *Hannibal* Creator Bryan Fuller on Dream Sequences, David Lynch, and FBI Consultants," *Reel Life with Jane*,

April 8, 2013, http://www.reellifewithjane.com/2013/04/exclusive-interview
-hannibal-creator-bryan-fuller-on-dream-sequences-david-lynch-fbi-consultants.

47 Author interview.

48 Lynch and Rodley, 184.

49 University of Southern California School of Cinematic Arts, *Twin Peaks*
Retrospective, May 5, 2013.

50 Author interview.

51 Author interview.

52 Joyce Millman, "Television/Radio; 'The X-Files' Finds the Truth: Its Time
Is Past," *New York Times*, May 19, 2002.

53 Rob Owen, "Tuned In: *Psych* Pays Tribute to *Twin Peaks*," *Pittsburgh Post-
Gazette*, November 28, 2010.

54 Radish.

55 Greg Olson, *David Lynch: Beautiful Dark* (Lanham, MD: Scarecrow Press,
2008), 301.

56 "Damon Lindelof discusses the personal impact of *Twin Peaks*," YouTube
video, from a TimesTalk Live, posted by holyvenom, June 20, 2010, https://
www.youtube.com/watch?v=jJBNk_Ii8jM.

57 Tim Stack, "EP Carlton Cuse: 'Bates Motel' is one part 'Friday Night
Lights,' one part 'Lost' and one part 'Twin Peaks,'" *Entertainment Weekly*,
March 18, 2013, http://insidetv.ew.com/2013/03/18/bates-motel-premiere.

58 Diane Haithman, "Carlton Cuse on *Bates Motel*'s *Twin Peaks* and *Psycho* Heritage," *Deadline*, May 10, 2013.

59 Tim Stack, "Exec producer Veena Sud spills secrets on TV's new hit mystery," *Entertainment Weekly*, April 17, 2011, http://insidetv.ew.com/ 2011/04/17/the-killing-executive-producer-secrets.

60 Author interview.

61 Author interview.

62 Author interview.

63 Author interview.

64 Author interview.

65 Author interview.

66 "Ray Wise Interview," by Ron Purtee, *The Ron Purtee Show*, episode 76, podcast audio, May 28, 2013, https://itunes.apple.com/ca/podcast/ episode-76-ray-wise/id513810450?i=160143587&mt=2.

Acknowledgments

A tip of the hat to the people who helped me along the way to what you now hold in your hands. First, thanks to the fine folks at ECW Press, including Sarah Dunn and Jenna Illies, who first suggested I send in a pitch for their Pop Classics line of books. Many thanks to my wonderful editors, Crissy Calhoun and Jennifer Knoch, for their faith in me and for allowing me the opportunity to write about something I've loved for so long.

Thanks to Jean-Paul Fallavollita, Glenn Walker, Luke Sneyd, and Marie Gilbert, my Biff Bam Pop crew, for keeping our little site that could running while I was in book-writing mode. Also thanks to my supportive colleagues at SiriusXM Canada, including Ward Anderson, Alison Dore, and Terry Mercury, who had me on their show to talk *Twin Peaks* as soon as they heard this book was coming.

While I was writing *Wrapped in Plastic*, I had the opportunity to also work with *Rue Morgue* magazine on their *Twin Peaks* cover story, which went to print in March 2014. Thanks to Dave Alexander for that opportunity and for his constant support.

A huge thank you to the various *Twin Peaks* actors and writers who took the time to talk to me for all my related projects: Jennifer Lynch, Kimmy Robertson, Robert Engels, Harley Peyton, Michael J. Anderson, James Marshall, Dana Ashbrook, Ian Buchanan, Ray Wise, and Sheryl Lee.

Finally, thanks to my family for their constant support — especially my wife, Jovanna, and my daughter, Anya, who for many months had to share me with the sycamore trees and the world of *Twin Peaks*. I love you both.